# NINJA 2025 DOUBLE STACK AIR FRYER

## Cookbook for Beginners

2000 Days Easy & Tasty Ninja Vertical Dual Drawer Air Fryer Recipe Book with Step-by-Step Cooking Tips to Simplify Your Cooking Journey

*Carriyulho Rguhlieiro*

Copyright© 2024 By Carriyulho Rguhlieiro

All rights reserved worldwide.

No part of this book may be reproduced or transmitted in any form or by any means, electronic or mechanical, including photo- copying, recording or by any information storage and retrieval system, without written permission from the publisher, except for the inclusion of brief quotations in a review.

Warning-Disclaimer

The purpose of this book is to educate and entertain. The author or publisher does not guarantee that anyone following the techniques, suggestions, tips, ideas, or strategies will become successful. The author and publisher shall have neither liability or responsibility to anyone with respect to any loss or damage caused, or alleged to be caused, directly or indirectly by the information contained in

# TABLE OF CONTENTS

| | | |
|---|---|---|
| 1 | Introduction | |
| 4 | Chapter 1 | Breakfasts |
| 14 | Chapter 2 | Family Favorites |
| 19 | Chapter 3 | Fast and Easy Everyday Favourites |
| 24 | Chapter 4 | Poultry |
| 38 | Chapter 5 | Beef, Pork, and Lamb |
| 48 | Chapter 6 | Fish and Seafood |
| 59 | Chapter 7 | Snacks and Starters |
| 68 | Chapter 8 | Vegetables and Sides |
| 76 | Chapter 9 | Vegetarian Mains |
| 81 | Chapter 10 | Desserts |
| 86 | Appendix 1: | Basic Kitchen Conversions & Equivalents |
| 87 | Appendix 2: | Recipes Index |

# INTRODUCTION

    Cooking has become an integral part of daily life, not just as a necessity but as an art form that brings families together and sparks creativity in the kitchen. This cookbook is designed to inspire and guide both novice and seasoned cooks on a flavorful journey, offering a comprehensive selection of recipes tailored for the Ninja Double Stack Air Fryer. With its unique vertical dual-drawer design, this versatile appliance simplifies the cooking process while delivering exceptional results. The recipes in this book have been meticulously crafted to help you unlock its full potential, creating meals that are as delicious as they are effortless.

    Inside, you'll discover 2000 days' worth of easy-to-follow recipes, ranging from hearty breakfasts to indulgent desserts. Each recipe includes detailed ingredient lists, precise measurements, cooking times, and step-by-step instructions. Whether you're preparing a quick snack, a full-course dinner, or a healthy alternative to traditional fried foods, this book ensures that every meal you make is a success.

# What You Can Expect?

**1. A Wealth of Recipes for Every Occasion:** This cookbook offers a vast array of options, ensuring there's something for everyone. You'll find recipes to suit every palate and dietary preference, from crispy appetizers and protein-rich mains to vegetarian sides and decadent sweets. The dishes are inspired by global cuisines, bringing a variety of flavors to your table and keeping your menu exciting and diverse. Whether it's a busy weeknight or a leisurely weekend gathering, the recipes are designed to make your life easier without compromising on taste.

**2. Simplified Cooking for Busy Lives:** Time is often a challenge in the kitchen, but this cookbook provides practical solutions. The recipes are written with simplicity in mind, featuring clear instructions that are easy to follow. With the Ninja Double Stack Air Fryer's dual drawers, you can cook multiple dishes simultaneously, making meal preparation faster and more efficient. Many recipes also include tips for pairing complementary dishes, allowing you to create balanced meals with minimal effort.

**3. Healthier Alternatives Without Sacrificing Flavor:** One of the greatest advantages of using an air fryer is the ability to enjoy your favorite fried foods with significantly less oil. This cookbook emphasizes health-conscious recipes that maintain the crispy textures and rich flavors you love. From golden-brown chicken wings to perfectly roasted vegetables, the recipes focus on fresh, wholesome ingredients that are as nourishing as they are delicious.

**4. Adaptability and Versatility:** The recipes in this book are designed to be versatile, allowing for easy substitutions and adjustments to suit your dietary needs and personal preferences. Whether you're cooking for a family, entertaining guests, or preparing meals for the week, the adaptable nature of these dishes ensures they fit seamlessly into your lifestyle. Variations and additional tips are included to help you customize each recipe and make it your own.

## Highlights of the Cookbook

**1. Efficient Use of Time:** The Ninja Double Stack Air Fryer is known for its ability to cook meals quickly and evenly, and the recipes in this book take full advantage of that feature. With precise cooking times and simple steps, you'll be able to spend less time in the kitchen and more time enjoying your meals.

**2. Meal Pairing Tips:** Cooking multiple dishes at once is made simple with the dual-drawer design. This book provides pairing suggestions, helping you coordinate flavors and textures for a well-rounded meal.

**3. Professional-Grade Results at Home:** Achieving restaurant-quality dishes has never been easier. The recipes are

tailored to maximize the capabilities of your air fryer, ensuring perfect results every time.

**4. A Resource for All Skill Levels:** Whether you're an experienced cook or a beginner just starting out, this book offers something for everyone. The detailed instructions and practical tips make it easy to get great results, regardless of your expertise.

# Why You'll Love This Cookbook?

This cookbook is more than just a collection of recipes—it's a tool for transforming your cooking habits. With its wide range of dishes and straightforward instructions, it makes cooking less daunting and more enjoyable. The thoughtfully designed recipes not only save you time but also inspire creativity in the kitchen, encouraging you to experiment with new ingredients and techniques.

Cooking with the Ninja Double Stack Air Fryer offers a unique opportunity to embrace healthier eating without sacrificing the flavors you love. This cookbook showcases the versatility of the appliance, guiding you through everything from quick snacks to elaborate meals. The step-by-step approach ensures that even complex dishes are easy to master, while the variety of recipes guarantees there's always something new to try.

Whether you're preparing a comforting family dinner, exploring global flavors, or impressing friends with your culinary skills, this cookbook is your ultimate guide. It simplifies the cooking process, enhances your results, and helps you create meals that bring joy to the table. With this collection of 2000 days' worth of recipes, you'll never run out of ideas or inspiration.

Let this cookbook be your trusted companion as you explore the endless possibilities of the Ninja Double Stack Air Fryer. From quick weeknight meals to weekend feasts, these recipes are here to simplify your cooking journey and make every dish a memorable one. Get ready to discover how easy and enjoyable home cooking can be!

# Chapter 1

## Breakfasts

# Chapter 1 Breakfasts

## Breakfast Meatballs

**Prep time: 10 minutes | Cook time: 15 minutes | Makes 18 meatballs**

- 450 g pork banger meat, removed from casings
- ½ teaspoon salt
- ¼ teaspoon ground black pepper
- 120 g grated mature Cheddar cheese
- 30 g soft cheese, softened
- 1 large egg, whisked

1. In a large bowl, combine all ingredients and mix thoroughly. Form the mixture into eighteen 1-inch meatballs.
2. Place the meatballs into Zone 1 and Zone 2 of the Ninja Double Stack Air Fryer basket, ensuring they are evenly spaced.
3. Select AIR FRY for both zones, set the temperature to 200°C, and set the timer to 15 minutes. Press MATCH to synchronize both zones and START/PAUSE to begin cooking.
4. Shake the baskets gently three times during cooking to ensure even browning. The meatballs will be browned on the outside and have an internal temperature of at least 64°C when fully cooked.
5. Once done, remove the meatballs from both zones and serve warm.

## Cinnamon-Raisin Bagels

**Prep time: 30 minutes | Cook time: 10 minutes | Makes 4 bagels**

- Oil, for spraying
- 60 g raisins
- 120 g self-raising flour, plus more for dusting
- 235 ml natural yoghurt
- 1 teaspoon ground cinnamon
- 1 large egg

1. Prepare the Ninja Double Stack Air Fryer baskets by lining them with parchment paper and lightly spraying with oil.
2. Soak the raisins in a bowl of hot water for 10 to 15 minutes until they plump up, making them extra juicy.
3. In a large mixing bowl, combine the flour, yogurt, and cinnamon. Use your hands or a silicone spatula to mix until a sticky dough ball forms.
4. Drain the soaked raisins and gently knead them into the dough until evenly distributed.
5. Transfer the dough onto a lightly floured surface and divide it into four equal portions. Roll each portion into an 8- to 9-inch rope and form it into a circle, pinching the ends to seal securely.
6. Whisk the egg in a small bowl and brush it over the tops of the dough circles.
7. Place two dough circles in each air fryer basket, ensuring they do not touch.
8. Set both Zone 1 and Zone 2 to 180°C and set the timer to 10 minutes. Select AIR FRY and pressing MATCH, then START/PAUSE

## Italian Egg Cups

**Prep time: 5 minutes | Cook time: 10 minutes | Serves 4**

- rapeseed oil
- 235 ml marinara sauce
- 4 eggs
- 4 tablespoons grated Cheddar cheese
- 4 teaspoons grated Parmesan cheese
- Salt and freshly ground black pepper, to taste
- Chopped fresh basil, for garnish

1. Lightly spray 4 individual ramekins with rapeseed oil to prevent sticking. Pour 60 ml of marinara sauce into each ramekin, creating an even base layer.
2. Crack one egg into each ramekin over the marinara sauce. Sprinkle 1 tablespoon of Mozzarella and 1 tablespoon of Parmesan cheese on top of each egg. Season with salt and pepper to taste.
3. Cover each ramekin with aluminum foil. Place two ramekins in Zone 1 of the Ninja Double Stack Air Fryer.
4. Air fry at 180°C for 5 minutes, then carefully remove the foil. Continue air frying for another 2 to 4 minutes, or until the top is lightly browned and the egg whites are set. If a firmer yolk is preferred, cook for an additional 3 to 5 minutes.
5. Repeat the process with the remaining two ramekins in Zone 2. Once done, garnish each ramekin with fresh basil and serve warm. Enjoy this flavorful and simple dish!

## Cinnamon Rolls

### Prep time: 10 minutes | Cook time: 20 minutes | Makes 12 rolls

- 600 g grated Cheddar cheese
- 60 g soft cheese, softened
- 120 g blanched finely ground almond flour
- ½ teaspoon vanilla extract
- 96 ml icing sugar-style sweetener
- 1 tablespoon ground cinnamon

1. In a large microwave-safe bowl, combine the Cheddar cheese, soft cheese, and flour. Microwave on high for 90 seconds, or until the cheese is fully melted. Stir the mixture thoroughly until smooth.
2. Add the vanilla extract and sweetener to the melted cheese mixture, mixing for about 2 minutes until a dough forms. Let the dough cool for approximately 2 minutes, or until it is comfortable to handle.
3. Spread the dough onto ungreased parchment paper, shaping it into a 12 × 4-inch rectangle. Evenly sprinkle the surface with cinnamon. Starting from the long edge, roll the dough tightly lengthwise to form a log. Slice the log into twelve equal pieces.
4. Divide the cinnamon rolls between two ungreased round nonstick baking dishes, ensuring the rolls are spaced slightly apart. Place one baking dish into Zone 1 of the Ninja Double Stack Air Fryer.
5. Set Zone 1 to 190ºC and bake for 10 minutes, or until the cinnamon rolls are golden brown around the edges and mostly firm. Repeat the same process with the second baking dish in Zone 2.
6. Allow the cinnamon rolls to cool in the baking dishes for about 10 minutes before serving. Enjoy the warm, gooey rolls fresh from the air fryer!

## Mississippi Spice Muffins

### Prep time: 15 minutes | Cook time: 13 minutes | Makes 12 muffins

- 1 kg plain
- 1 tablespoon ground cinnamon
- 2 teaspoons baking soda
- 2 teaspoons allspice
- 1 teaspoon ground cloves
- 1 teaspoon salt
- 235 g (2 sticks) butter, room temperature
- 350 g sugar
- 2 large eggs, lightly beaten
- 475 ml unsweetened apple sauce
- 60 g chopped pecans
- 1 to 2 tablespoons oil

1. In a large bowl, whisk together the flour, cinnamon, baking soda, allspice, cloves, and salt until the mixture is evenly blended.
2. In another large bowl, combine the butter and sugar. Use an electric mixer to beat the mixture for 2 to 3 minutes until it becomes light and fluffy. Add the beaten eggs and stir until fully incorporated.
3. Gradually add the flour mixture and applesauce to the butter mixture, alternating between the two and blending after each addition until a smooth batter forms. Fold in the pecans, ensuring they are evenly distributed.
4. Preheat Zone 1 and Zone 2 to 160ºC. Lightly spritz 12 silicone muffin cups with oil to prevent sticking.
5. Divide the batter evenly among the prepared muffin cups, filling each halfway. Place six muffin cups in Zone 1 and the remaining six in Zone 2, ensuring they are arranged in a single layer.
6. Air fry the muffins for 6 minutes. Shake the baskets gently and continue air frying for an additional 7 minutes, or until a toothpick inserted into the center of a muffin comes out clean.
7. Carefully remove the muffins from the air fryer and allow them to cool slightly before serving. Enjoy your delicious spiced muffins warm or at room temperature!

## Quesadillas

### Prep time: 10 minutes | Cook time: 15 minutes | Serves 4

- 4 eggs
- 2 tablespoons skimmed milk
- Salt and pepper, to taste
- Oil for misting or cooking spray
- 4 wheat maize wraps
- 4 tablespoons tomato salsa
- 60 g Cheddar cheese, grated
- ½ small avocado, peeled and thinly sliced

1. Preheat both Zone 1 and Zone 2 of the Ninja Double Stack Air Fryer to 130ºC by selecting AIR FRY and pressing MATCH, then START/PAUSE.
2. In a medium bowl, beat together the eggs, milk, salt, and pepper until well combined.
3. Lightly spray a baking pan with cooking spray and pour the egg mixture into the pan.
4. Place the pan into Zone 1 and bake for 8 to 9 minutes, stirring every 1 to 2 minutes, until the eggs are scrambled to your liking. Once done, remove the pan and set the scrambled eggs aside.
5. Spray one side of each maize wrap with oil or cooking spray. Flip the wraps over.
6. Divide the scrambled eggs, tomato salsa, cheese, and avocado among the maize wraps, covering only half of each wrap.
7. Fold each wrap in half and press down lightly to secure.
8. Place two maize wraps into Zone 1 and two into Zone 2 of the air fryer basket. Select AIR FRY at 200ºC and set the timer for 3 minutes. Press MATCH to synchronize both zones and START/PAUSE to begin cooking. Cook until the cheese melts and the outside feels slightly crispy.
10. Once done, remove the wraps from both zones and cut each into halves or thirds.

## Nutty Muesli

**Prep time: 5 minutes | Cook time: 1 hour | Serves 4**

- 120 g pecans, roughly chopped
- 120 g walnuts or almonds, roughly chopped
- 60 g desiccated coconut
- 30 g almond flour
- 60 g ground flaxseed or chia seeds
- 2 tablespoons sunflower seeds
- 2 tablespoons melted butter
- 60 ml granulated sweetener
- ½ teaspoon ground cinnamon
- ½ teaspoon vanilla extract
- ¼ teaspoon ground nutmeg
- ¼ teaspoon salt
- 2 tablespoons water

1. Preheat both Zone 1 and Zone 2 to 190°C by selecting AIR FRY and pressing MATCH, then START/PAUSE. In a large mixing bowl, combine the turkey, garlic, onion, Tabasco, Cajun seasoning, thyme, paprika, and cayenne. Use clean hands to mix the ingredients thoroughly until evenly incorporated. Shape the mixture into 16 patties, each about ½ inch thick. If the mixture feels too sticky, slightly wet your hands to make shaping easier.
2. Arrange eight patties in Zone 1 and the remaining eight in Zone 2, ensuring they are laid in a single layer with enough space for air circulation.
3. Air fry the patties for 15 to 20 minutes, pausing halfway through the cooking time to flip them for even browning. The patties are done when a thermometer inserted into the thickest part reads 74°C. Remove the cooked patties, serve warm, and enjoy their flavorful, juicy goodness!

## Quick and Easy Blueberry Muffins

**Prep time: 10 minutes | Cook time: 12 minutes | Makes 8 muffins**

- 160 g flour
- 96 g sugar
- 2 teaspoons baking powder
- ¼ teaspoon salt
- 80 ml rapeseed oil
- 1 egg
- 120 ml milk
- 160 g blueberries, fresh or frozen and thawed

1. Preheat both Zone 1 and Zone 2 to 170°C by selecting AIR FRY and pressing MATCH, then START/PAUSE. In a medium bowl, mix together the flour, sugar, baking powder, and salt until evenly combined.
2. In a separate bowl, whisk the oil, egg, and milk until well blended. Gradually pour this mixture into the dry ingredients and stir gently until just moistened, being careful not to overmix.
3. Fold the blueberries into the batter, ensuring they are evenly distributed. Line muffin cups with parchment paper and spoon the batter evenly into eight prepared cups.
4. Place four filled muffin cups in Zone 1 and the other four in Zone 2. Bake for 12 minutes, or until the tops spring back when lightly touched and a toothpick inserted in the center comes out clean.
5. Carefully remove the muffins from the air fryer, allow them to cool for a few minutes, and serve immediately for the best flavor and texture. Enjoy your freshly baked blueberry muffins!

## Bacon, Broccoli and Cheese Bread Pudding

**Prep time: 30 minutes | Cook time: 48 minutes | Serves 2 to 4**

- 230 g streaky bacon, cut into ¼-inch pieces
- 700 g brioche bread or rolls, cut into ½-inch cubes
- 3 eggs
- 235 ml milk
- ½ teaspoon salt
- freshly ground black pepper
- 235 g frozen broccoli florets, thawed and chopped
- 350 g grated Emmental cheese

1. Preheat both Zone 1 and Zone 2 to 200°C by selecting AIR FRY and pressing MATCH, then START/PAUSE. Place the bacon in the baskets and air fry for 6 to 10 minutes, shaking the baskets a few times to ensure even cooking. Once crispy, remove the bacon and place it on a paper towel to drain.
2. Spread the brioche bread cubes evenly across the baskets and air fry for 2 minutes to dry and toast them lightly. If the brioche is slightly stale, this step can be skipped.
3. Butter two cake pans and set them aside. In a large mixing bowl, combine the toasted bread cubes, crispy bacon, and the remaining ingredients. Toss everything together until well mixed. Divide the mixture evenly between the two buttered cake pans. Cover the pans tightly with aluminum foil and refrigerate for at least 8 hours or overnight to allow the flavors to meld.
4. Remove the pans from the refrigerator about an hour before cooking to allow the mixture to come to room temperature. Preheat both zones of the air fryer to 170°C.
5. Create slings by folding two pieces of aluminum foil into 2-inch-wide, 24-inch-long strips. Use the slings to lower the pans into the baskets, folding the ends of the foil over the top of the pans to keep them secure. Air fry the covered pans for 20 minutes.
6. Remove the foil from the pans and continue air frying for an additional 20 minutes. If the tops begin to brown too quickly before the custard sets, loosely place the foil back over the pans. The bread pudding is fully cooked when a skewer inserted into the center comes out clean. Allow to cool slightly before serving. Enjoy!

# Eggnog Bread

### Prep time: 10 minutes | Cook time: 18 minutes | Serves 6 to 8

- 120 g flour, plus more for dusting
- 35 g sugar
- 1 teaspoon baking powder
- ¼ teaspoon salt
- ¼ teaspoon nutmeg
- 120 ml eggnog
- 1 egg yolk
- 1 tablespoon plus 1 teaspoon butter, melted
- 60 g pecans
- 60 g chopped candied fruit (cherries, pineapple, or mixed fruits)
- Cooking spray

1. Preheat both Zone 1 and Zone 2 to 180ºC by selecting AIR FRY and pressing MATCH, then START/PAUSE. In a medium bowl, combine the flour, sugar, baking powder, salt, and nutmeg, stirring until evenly mixed.
2. Add the eggnog, egg yolk, and melted butter to the dry ingredients. Mix gently until just combined, being careful not to overmix.
3. Fold in the nuts and dried fruit, ensuring they are evenly distributed throughout the batter.
4. Spray two small air fryer-safe baking dishes with cooking spray and lightly dust with flour to prevent sticking.
5. Divide the batter evenly between the prepared baking dishes, spreading it out smoothly.
6. Place one baking dish in Zone 1 and the other in Zone 2. Bake for 18 minutes, or until the tops are dark golden brown and the edges begin to pull away from the sides of the pans.
7. Carefully remove the dishes from the air fryer, allow to cool for a few minutes, then slice and serve immediately. Enjoy this warm and flavorful treat!

# Peppered Maple Bacon Knots

### Prep time: 5 minutes | Cook time: 7 to 8 minutes | Serves 6

- 450 g maple smoked/cured bacon rashers
- 60 ml maple syrup
- 48 g soft brown sugar
- Coarsely cracked black peppercorns, to taste

1. Preheat both Zone 1 and Zone 2 to 200ºC by selecting AIR FRY and pressing MATCH, then START/PAUSE. On a clean work surface, take each bacon strip and tie it into a loose knot, ensuring the ends are tucked neatly.
2. In a small bowl, mix together the maple syrup and soft brown sugar until smooth. Generously brush this sweet glaze over the prepared bacon knots, coating them evenly.
3. Arrange half of the bacon knots in Zone 1 and the other half in Zone 2, placing them in a single layer to avoid overcrowding. Sprinkle the knots with coarsely cracked black peppercorns for an added kick of flavor.
4. Air fry the bacon knots for 5 minutes. Carefully flip each knot, then continue cooking for an additional 2 to 3 minutes, or until the bacon becomes crisp and caramelized.
5. Remove the cooked bacon knots and transfer them to a plate lined with paper towels to absorb any excess grease. Repeat the process for any remaining bacon knots if needed.
6. Allow the bacon knots to cool for a few minutes before serving. Serve warm and enjoy these flavorful, crispy treats!

# Oat Bran Muffins

### Prep time: 10 minutes | Cook time: 10 to 12 minutes per batch | Makes 8 muffins

- 160 g oat bran
- 60 g flour
- 45 g soft brown sugar
- 1 teaspoon baking powder
- ½ teaspoon baking soda
- ⅛ teaspoon salt
- 120 ml buttermilk
- 1 egg
- 2 tablespoons rapeseed oil
- 120 g chopped dates, raisins, or dried cranberries
- 24 paper muffin cases
- Cooking spray

1. Preheat both Zone 1 and Zone 2 of the Ninja Double Stack Air Fryer to 130ºC by selecting AIR FRY and pressing MATCH, then START/PAUSE.
2. In a medium bowl, beat together the eggs, milk, salt, and pepper until well combined.
3. Lightly spray a baking pan with cooking spray and pour the egg mixture into the pan.
4. Place the pan into Zone 1 and bake for 8 to 9 minutes, stirring every 1 to 2 minutes, until the eggs are scrambled to your liking. Once done, remove the pan and set the scrambled eggs aside.
5. Spray one side of each maize wrap with oil or cooking spray. Flip the wraps over.
6. Divide the scrambled eggs, tomato salsa, cheese, and avocado among the maize wraps, covering only half of each wrap.
7. Fold each wrap in half and press down lightly to secure.
8. Place two maize wraps into Zone 1 and two into Zone 2 of the air fryer basket. Select AIR FRY at 200ºC and set the timer for 3 minutes. Press MATCH to synchronize both zones and START/PAUSE to begin cooking. Cook until the cheese melts and the outside feels slightly crispy.
9. Once done, remove the wraps from both zones and cut each into halves or thirds.

## Kale and Potato Nuggets

**Prep time: 10 minutes | Cook time: 18 minutes | Serves 4**

- 1 teaspoon extra virgin rapeseed oil
- 1 clove garlic, minced
- 1 kg kale, rinsed and chopped
- 475 g potatoes, boiled and mashed
- 30 ml milk
- Salt and ground black pepper, to taste
- Cooking spray

1. Preheat Zone 1 and Zone 2 to 200ºC.
2. In a frying pan over medium heat, sauté the garlic in rapeseed oil until golden brown. Add the kale and sauté for an additional 3 minutes, then remove from the heat and let it cool slightly.
3. In a mixing bowl, combine the mashed potatoes, sautéed kale, and garlic. Pour in the milk, season with salt and pepper, and mix until well combined.
4. Shape the mixture into small nugget-sized pieces and lightly spritz them with cooking spray to ensure crispiness.
5. Place half of the nuggets in Zone 1 and the other half in Zone 2. Air fry for 15 minutes, flipping the nuggets halfway through to ensure even cooking on all sides.
6. Once golden and crispy, remove the nuggets and serve immediately. Enjoy these savory bites while they're warm!

## Double-Dipped Mini Cinnamon Biscuits

**Prep time: 15 minutes | Cook time: 13 minutes | Makes 8 biscuits**

- 240g blanched almond flour
- 60 g powdered sweetener
- 1 teaspoon baking powder
- ½ teaspoon fine sea salt
- 60 g plus 2 tablespoons (¾ stick) very cold unsalted butter
- 60 ml unsweetened, unflavoured almond milk
- 1 large egg
- 1 teaspoon vanilla extract
- 3 teaspoons ground cinnamon

Glaze:
- 60 g powdered sweetener
- 60 ml double cream or unsweetened, unflavoured almond milk

1. Preheat Zone 1 and Zone 2 to 180ºC. Line two pie dishes that fit into the baskets with parchment paper.
2. In a medium bowl, combine the almond flour, sweetener (if powdered; avoid using liquid sweetener), baking powder, and salt. Cut the butter into ½-inch squares and use a hand mixer to incorporate it into the dry ingredients. The mixture should remain slightly chunky with visible pieces of butter.
3. In a separate small bowl, whisk together the almond milk, egg, and vanilla extract (add liquid sweetener here if using). Pour the wet ingredients into the dry mixture and use a fork to stir until large clumps form. Add the cinnamon and gently swirl it into the dough using your hands.
4. Divide the dough into sixteen 1-inch balls. Arrange half of the balls in one prepared pie dish and the other half in the second dish, spacing them about ½ inch apart. Place one dish in Zone 1 and the other in Zone 2. Bake for 10 to 13 minutes, or until the biscuits turn golden brown. Remove the dishes from the air fryer and let the biscuits cool in the pans for at least 5 minutes.
5. While the biscuits bake, prepare the glaze. In a small bowl, combine the powdered sweetener and double cream. Slowly stir with a fork until smooth.
6. Once the biscuits have cooled slightly, dip the tops into the glaze, allow them to dry for a moment, then dip again to create a thick coating.
7. Serve the biscuits warm or at room temperature. Store any unglazed biscuits in an airtight container in the refrigerator for up to 3 days or freeze for up to 1 month. To reheat, place them in the preheated air fryer at 180ºC for 5 minutes or until warmed through. Dip in the glaze as desired before serving.

## Jalapeño and Bacon Breakfast Pizza

**Prep time: 5 minutes | Cook time: 10 minutes | Serves 2**

- 235 ml grated Cheddar cheese
- 30 g soft cheese, broken into small pieces
- 4 slices cooked bacon, chopped
- 60 g chopped pickled jalapeños
- 1 large egg, whisked
- ¼ teaspoon salt

1. Place the Mozzarella in a single layer at the bottom of an ungreased round nonstick baking dish. Scatter the soft cheese pieces, bacon, and jalapeños evenly over the Mozzarella, then pour the beaten egg mixture evenly around the baking dish.
2. Sprinkle the top with salt and place the baking dish into Zone 1 of the Ninja Double Stack Air Fryer. Set the temperature to 170ºC and bake for 10 minutes. The pizza is done when the cheese is browned and the egg is fully set.
3. Carefully remove the baking dish from Zone 1 and transfer the pizza onto a large plate. Let it cool for about 5 minutes before slicing and serving. Enjoy!

## Bourbon Vanilla Eggy Bread

**Prep time: 15 minutes | Cook time: 6 minutes | Serves 4**

- 2 large eggs
- 2 tablespoons water
- 160 ml whole or semi-skimmed milk
- 1 tablespoon butter, melted
- 2 tablespoons bourbon
- 1 teaspoon vanilla extract
- 8 (1-inch-thick) French bread slices
- Cooking spray

1. Preheat Zone 1 and Zone 2 to 160ºC. Line each basket with parchment paper and lightly spray with cooking spray to prevent sticking.
2. In a shallow bowl, beat the eggs with the water until combined. Add the milk, melted butter, bourbon, and vanilla, stirring until the mixture is smooth and well blended.
3. Dip 4 slices of bread into the batter, ensuring both sides are evenly coated. Place the slices onto the parchment paper in Zone 1.
4. Air fry for 6 minutes, flipping the slices halfway through to ensure even browning. Once done, transfer the cooked slices to a plate.
5. Repeat the process with the remaining 4 slices of bread in Zone 2, following the same steps.
6. Serve the warm French toast immediately, and enjoy!

## Hearty Blueberry Porridge

**Prep time: 10 minutes | Cook time: 25 minutes | Serves 6**

- 350 g porridge oats
- 1¼ teaspoons ground cinnamon, divided
- ½ teaspoon baking powder
- Pinch salt
- 235 ml unsweetened vanilla almond milk
- 60 ml honey
- 1 teaspoon vanilla extract
- 1 egg, beaten
- 475 g blueberries
- vegetable oil (such as rapeseed oil)
- 1½ teaspoons sugar, divided
- 6 tablespoons low-fat whipped topping (optional)

1. In a large bowl, combine the oats, 1 teaspoon of cinnamon, baking powder, and salt, mixing well. In a medium bowl, whisk together the almond milk, honey, vanilla, and egg until smooth. Pour the liquid mixture into the dry ingredients and stir until fully combined. Gently fold in the blueberries.
2. Lightly spray two baking pans with oil. Divide the blueberry mixture evenly between the pans, spreading half into each one. Sprinkle ⅛ teaspoon of cinnamon and ½ teaspoon of sugar over the top of the mixture in each pan.
3. Cover both pans with aluminum foil. Place one pan in Zone 1 and the other in Zone 2. Preheat both zones to 180ºC and air fry the covered pans for 20 minutes.
4. Remove the foil and continue air frying for an additional 5 minutes, or until the top is golden and the mixture is set. Carefully remove the pans from the air fryer and transfer the baked mixture to shallow bowls.
5. To serve, spoon into individual bowls and top with whipped topping. Enjoy this warm and comforting treat!

## Fried Chicken Wings with Waffles

**Prep time: 10 minutes | Cook time: 30 minutes | Serves 4**

- 8 whole chicken wings
- 1 teaspoon garlic powder
- Chicken seasoning, for preparing the chicken
- Freshly ground black pepper, to taste
- 60 g plain flour
- Cooking oil spray
- 8 frozen waffles
- Pure maple syrup, for serving (optional)

1. In a medium bowl, combine the chicken and garlic powder, then season with chicken seasoning and pepper. Toss to coat evenly. Transfer the seasoned chicken to a resealable plastic bag, add the flour, seal the bag, and shake it thoroughly to coat the chicken.
2. Preheat Zone 1 and Zone 2 to 200ºC by selecting AIR FRY and pressing MATCH, then START/PAUSE. Spray both baskets with cooking oil. Using tongs, transfer the coated chicken from the bag into the baskets, dividing it evenly between Zone 1 and Zone 2. It is acceptable to stack the chicken wings slightly. Spray the chicken with cooking oil for a crispy finish.
3. Air fry the chicken at 200ºC for 20 minutes, shaking the baskets every 5 minutes to ensure even cooking. The chicken is fully cooked when golden brown and crispy. Remove the chicken from the baskets, cover it to keep warm, and set aside.
4. Rinse both baskets and crisper plates with warm water, then reinsert them into Zone 1 and Zone 2. Preheat both zones to 180ºC.
5. Once preheated, spray the crisper plates with cooking spray. Working in batches, place the frozen waffles in the baskets, ensuring they are arranged in a single layer without stacking. Spray the waffles lightly with cooking oil.
6. Air fry the waffles at 180ºC for 6 minutes, checking halfway through to ensure even toasting. Remove the cooked waffles and repeat the process with any remaining batches.
7. Serve the crispy chicken alongside the waffles. Add a drizzle of maple syrup if desired for a sweet and savory touch. Enjoy this comforting and delicious meal!

## Mushroom-and-Tomato Stuffed Hash Browns

**Prep time: 10 minutes | Cook time: 20 minutes | Serves 4**

- rapeseed oil cooking spray
- 1 tablespoon plus 2 teaspoons rapeseed oil, divided
- 110 g baby mushrooms, diced
- 1 spring onion, white parts and green parts, diced
- 1 garlic clove, minced
- 475 g grated potatoes
- ½ teaspoon salt
- ¼ teaspoon black pepper
- 1 plum tomato, diced
- 120 g grated mozzarella

1. Preheat both Zone 1 and Zone 2 to 190°C. Lightly coat the inside of two 6-inch cake pans with rapeseed oil cooking spray.
2. Heat 2 teaspoons of rapeseed oil in a small frying pan over medium heat. Add the mushrooms, spring onion, and garlic, cooking for 4 to 5 minutes until softened and lightly browned. Remove from heat and set aside.
3. In a large bowl, combine the potatoes with salt, pepper, and the remaining tablespoon of rapeseed oil, tossing until evenly coated.
4. Divide half of the potatoes between the two prepared cake pans, spreading them evenly to form a base layer. Top each layer with the cooked mushroom mixture, tomato slices, and mozzarella cheese, then evenly spread the remaining potatoes over the top to cover.
5. Place one cake pan in Zone 1 and the other in Zone 2. Bake at 190°C for 12 to 15 minutes, or until the tops are golden brown and crispy.
6. Carefully remove the cake pans from the air fryer and let them cool for 5 minutes before slicing and serving. Enjoy your delicious layered potato bake!

## Oat and Chia Porridge

**Prep time: 10 minutes | Cook time: 5 minutes | Serves 4**

- 2 tablespoons peanut butter
- 4 tablespoons honey
- 1 tablespoon butter, melted
- 1 L milk
- 475 g oats
- 235 g chia seeds

1. Preheat Zone 1 and Zone 2 to 200°C.
2. In a mixing bowl, combine the peanut butter, honey, butter, and milk. Stir until smooth and well blended. Add the oats and chia seeds, mixing until all ingredients are evenly coated.
3. Divide the mixture into two small air fryer-safe bowls. Place one bowl in Zone 1 and the other in Zone 2.
4. Air fry at 200°C for 5 minutes. Once cooked, remove the bowls and stir the mixture to distribute the heat evenly. Serve warm and enjoy!

## Parmesan Ranch Risotto & Frico

**Prep time: 10 minutes | Cook time: 30 minutes**

### Parmesan Ranch Risotto | Serves 2

- 1 tablespoon rapeseed oil
- 1 clove garlic, minced
- 1 tablespoon unsalted butter
- 1 onion, diced
- 180 g Arborio rice
- 475 g chicken stock, boiling
- 120 g Parmesan cheese, grated

### Frico | Serves 2

- 235 g shredded aged Manchego cheese
- 1 teaspoon plain flour
- ½ teaspoon cumin seeds
- ¼ teaspoon cracked black pepper

**For Parmesan Ranch Risotto:**

1. Preheat Zone 1 to 200°C. Grease a round baking tin with rapeseed oil and stir in the garlic, butter, and onion.
2. Place the prepared tin into Zone 1 and bake for 4 minutes. Add the rice to the tin, stir well, and bake for an additional 4 minutes.
3. Reduce the temperature of Zone 1 to 160°C. Pour the chicken stock into the tin, cover it with aluminum foil, and bake for 22 minutes, or until the rice is tender and the stock is fully absorbed.
4. Remove the tin from Zone 1, uncover, and scatter cheese over the top. Serve immediately while warm and enjoy!

**For Frico:**

1. Preheat Zone 2 to 190°C. Line the basket with parchment paper to prevent sticking.
2. In a bowl, combine the cheese and flour. Stir thoroughly to mix until evenly combined. Spread the mixture into a 4-inch round on the parchment paper in the basket.
3. In a small bowl, mix the cumin and black pepper together until well blended. Sprinkle this seasoning mixture evenly over the cheese round.
4. Air fry in Zone 2 for 5 minutes, or until the cheese is lightly browned and frothy.
5. Carefully use tongs to transfer the cheese wafer to a plate. Slice into pieces and serve while warm or at room temperature. Enjoy this crispy and flavorful snack!

# Egg White Cups

**Prep time: 10 minutes | Cook time: 15 minutes | Serves 4**

- 475 ml 100% liquid egg whites
- 3 tablespoons salted butter, melted
- ¼ teaspoon salt
- ¼ teaspoon onion granules
- ½ medium plum tomato, cored and diced
- 120 g chopped fresh spinach leaves

1. In a large bowl, whisk the egg whites with melted butter, salt, and onion granules until well combined. Stir in the chopped tomato and spinach. Divide the mixture evenly among four ramekins greased with cooking spray.
2. Preheat Zone 1 and Zone 2 to 150°C. Place two ramekins into Zone 1 and the other two into Zone 2.
3. Air fry at 150°C for 15 minutes, or until the eggs are fully cooked and firm in the center.
4. Carefully remove the ramekins from both zones and allow them to cool slightly. Serve the baked egg cups warm and enjoy!

# Ham and Cheese Crescents

**Prep time: 5 minutes | Cook time: 7 minutes | Makes 8 rolls**

- Oil, for spraying
- 1 (230 g) tin ready-to-bake croissants
- 4 slices wafer-thin gammon
- 8 cheese slices
- 2 tablespoons unsalted butter, melted

1. Line both baskets with parchment paper and spray lightly with oil to prevent sticking.
2. Separate the dough into 8 equal pieces, ensuring they are evenly sized.
3. Tear the gammon slices in half and place one piece of gammon on each dough portion. Top each with a slice of cheese, ensuring the fillings are evenly distributed.
4. Roll up each piece of dough, starting from the wider side, and tuck the ends gently to secure the filling.
5. Arrange four rolls in each prepared basket, leaving some space between them for even cooking. Brush the tops of the rolls with melted butter for added flavor and color.
6. Set both zones to 160°C and air fry for 6 to 7 minutes, or until the rolls are puffed, golden brown, and the cheese inside is melted. Carefully remove the rolls and serve warm. Enjoy!

# Berry Muffins

**Prep time: 15 minutes | Cook time: 12 to 17 minutes | Makes 8 muffins**

- 160 g plus 1 tablespoon plain flour, divided
- 48 g granulated sugar
- 2 tablespoons light soft brown sugar
- 2 teaspoons baking powder
- 2 eggs
- 160 ml whole milk
- 80 ml neutral oil
- 235 g mixed fresh berries

1. In a medium bowl, mix 315 g of flour, granulated sugar, soft brown sugar, and baking powder until well combined. In a separate small bowl, whisk together the eggs, milk, and oil until smooth. Stir the wet mixture into the dry ingredients, mixing just until combined.
2. In another small bowl, toss the mixed berries with 1 tablespoon of flour to coat them evenly. Gently fold the berries into the batter, being careful not to overmix.
3. Double up 16 foil muffin cups to create 8 sturdy cups. Divide them equally between Zone 1 and Zone 2. Preheat both zones to 160°C.
4. Once preheated, fill the muffin cups in Zone 1 and Zone 2 three-quarters full with the batter. Air fry at 160°C for 17 minutes.
5. After 12 minutes, check the muffins in both zones. Lightly touch the tops with your finger; if they spring back, they are done. If not, continue cooking for the remaining time.
6. When the muffins are done, transfer them to a wire rack to cool. Repeat the process with any remaining batter, ensuring all muffins are baked evenly.
7. Allow the muffins to cool for 10 minutes before serving. Enjoy these fluffy, berry-packed treats!

# Pancake Cake

**Prep time: 10 minutes | Cook time: 7 minutes | Serves 4**

- 60 g blanched finely ground almond flour
- 30 g powdered erythritol
- ½ teaspoon baking powder
- 2 tablespoons unsalted butter, softened
- 1 large egg
- ½ teaspoon unflavoured gelatin
- ½ teaspoon vanilla extract
- ½ teaspoon ground cinnamon

1. In a large bowl, mix the almond flour, erythritol, and baking powder until combined. Add the butter, egg, gelatin, vanilla, and cinnamon, stirring until the batter is smooth. Divide the batter evenly between two round baking pans, spreading it out smoothly in each pan.
2. Preheat Zone 1 and Zone 2 to 150°C. Place one prepared pan in Zone 1 and the other in Zone 2.
3. Air fry both pans at 150°C for 7 minutes. Check for doneness by inserting a toothpick into the center of each cake; they are ready when the toothpick comes out clean.
4. Carefully remove the pans from both zones and let the cakes cool slightly. Slice each cake into four portions and serve. Enjoy these perfectly baked treats warm or at room temperature!

# Chapter 2
## Family Favorites

# Chapter 2 Family Favorites

## Veggie Tuna Toasties

**Prep time: 15 minutes | Cook time: 7 to 11 minutes | Serves 4**

- 2 low-salt wholemeal English muffins, split
- 1 (170 g) tin chunk light low-salt tuna, drained
- 235 g shredded carrot
- 80 g chopped mushrooms
- 2 spring onions, white and green parts, sliced
- 80 ml fat-free Greek yoghurt
- 2 tablespoons low-salt wholegrain mustard
- 2 slices low-salt low-fat Swiss cheese, halved

1. Place the English muffin halves in Zone 1 and Zone 2 of the Ninja Double Stack Air Fryer.
2. Air fry at 170ºC for 3 to 4 minutes, or until the muffins are crisp. Remove them from the baskets and set aside.
3. In a medium bowl, mix the tuna, carrot, mushrooms, spring onions, yoghurt, and mustard until thoroughly combined.
4. Spread one-fourth of the tuna mixture onto each muffin half, then top with half a slice of Swiss cheese.
5. Return the topped muffins to Zone 1 and Zone 2, and air fry for 4 to 7 minutes at 170ºC, or until the tuna mixture is heated through and the cheese melts and begins to brown.
6. Remove from the air fryer and serve immediately. Enjoy these delicious tuna melts!

## Mixed Berry Crumble Delight

**Prep time: 10 minutes | Cook time: 11 to 16 minutes | Serves 4**

- 120 g chopped fresh strawberries
- 120 g fresh blueberries
- 80 g frozen raspberries
- 1 tablespoon freshly squeezed lemon juice
- 1 tablespoon honey
- 80 g wholemeal plain flour
- 3 tablespoons light muscovado sugar
- 2 tablespoons unsalted butter, melted

1. In a baking pan, combine the strawberries, blueberries, and raspberries, spreading them evenly across the bottom.
2. Drizzle the fruit with lemon juice and honey, ensuring the berries are lightly coated.
3. In a small bowl, mix the pastry flour and brown sugar until combined. Add the butter and stir until the mixture becomes crumbly.
4. Evenly sprinkle the crumble mixture over the fruit, covering the berries completely.
5. Preheat Zone 1 and Zone 2 to 190ºC. Place the baking pan into Zone 1 and bake for 11 to 16 minutes, or until the fruit is tender, bubbly, and the topping is golden brown.
6. Carefully remove the pan from the air fryer, let it cool slightly, and serve the mixed berry crumble warm. Enjoy!

## Savory Pork Burgers with Tangy Red Cabbage Slaw

**Prep time: 20 minutes | Cook time: 7 to 9 minutes | Serves 4**

- 120 ml Greek yoghurt
- 2 tablespoons low-salt mustard, divided
- 1 tablespoon lemon juice
- 60 g sliced red cabbage
- 60 g grated carrots
- 450 g lean finely chopped pork
- ½ teaspoon paprika
- 235 g mixed salad leaves
- 2 small tomatoes, sliced
- 8 small low-salt wholemeal sandwich buns, cut in half

1. In a small bowl, combine the yoghurt, 1 tablespoon of mustard, lemon juice, cabbage, and carrots. Mix well, cover, and refrigerate to let the flavors meld.
2. In a medium bowl, mix the pork with the remaining 1 tablespoon of mustard and paprika. Divide the mixture evenly and shape it into 8 small patties.
3. Preheat Zone 1 and Zone 2 to 200ºC. Place 4 patties in Zone 1 and the other 4 patties in Zone 2, ensuring they are arranged in a single layer for even cooking.
4. Air fry the patties for 7 to 9 minutes, flipping them halfway through. Use a meat thermometer to ensure they reach an internal temperature of 74ºC.
5. Assemble the burgers by placing lettuce greens on the bottom half of each bun, followed by a tomato slice, one pork patty, and a generous spoonful of the chilled cabbage mixture.
6. Top with the other half of the bun, serve immediately, and enjoy these flavorful pork sliders!

## Creamy Mushroom and Green Bean Bake

**Prep time: 10 minutes | Cook time: 15 minutes | Serves 4**

- 4 tablespoons unsalted butter
- 60 g diced brown onion
- 120 g chopped white mushrooms
- 120 ml double cream
- 30 g full fat soft white cheese
- 120 g chicken broth
- ¼ teaspoon xanthan gum
- 450 g fresh green beans, edges trimmed
- 14 g pork crackling, finely ground

1. In a medium skillet over medium heat, melt the butter. Add the onion and mushrooms, and sauté for 3 to 5 minutes, or until soft and fragrant.
2. Stir in the double cream, soft white cheese, and broth. Whisk the mixture until smooth, then bring it to a boil before reducing to a simmer. Sprinkle in the xanthan gum and remove the skillet from the heat, stirring until the sauce thickens slightly.
3. Preheat Zone 1 and Zone 2 to 160°C.
4. Chop the green beans into 2-inch pieces and place them in a baking dish. Pour the prepared sauce over the green beans and stir until they are evenly coated.
5. Sprinkle the minced pork crackling evenly over the top of the dish. Place the baking dish into Zone 1 and bake for 15 minutes.
6. The dish is ready when the topping is golden and the green beans are fork-tender. Carefully remove the baking dish from Zone 1 and serve the casserole warm. Enjoy this creamy, flavorful side dish!

## Cinnamon Apple Egg Rolls

**Prep time: 10 minutes | Cook time: 8 minutes | Makes 6 rolls**

- Oil, for spraying
- 1 (600 g) tin apple pie filling
- 1 tablespoon plain flour
- ½ teaspoon lemon juice
- ¼ teaspoon ground nutmeg
- ¼ teaspoon ground cinnamon
- 6 egg roll wrappers

1. Preheat Zone 1 and Zone 2 to 200°C. Line each basket with parchment paper and lightly spray with oil to prevent sticking.
2. In a medium bowl, combine the pie filling, flour, lemon juice, nutmeg, and cinnamon, mixing until well combined.
3. Lay out the egg roll wrappers on a clean work surface. Spoon a dollop of the pie filling mixture into the center of each wrapper.
4. Fill a small bowl with water. Dip your finger in the water and moisten the edges of one wrapper at a time. Fold the wrapper like a packet: first fold one corner into the center, then fold each side corner inward, and finally fold over the remaining corner, ensuring the edges overlap. Press gently to seal.
5. Use additional water as needed to seal any open edges. Repeat the process with the remaining wrappers.
6. Place half of the prepared rolls into Zone 1 and the other half into Zone 2, arranging them in a single layer. Spray the rolls liberally with oil to ensure crispiness.
7. Air fry for 4 minutes. Open the baskets, flip the rolls, spray them with oil, and cook for another 4 minutes, or until the rolls are golden brown and crispy.
8. Remove the rolls from the baskets and serve immediately. Enjoy these warm, flaky treats!

## Crispy Filo Vegetable Parcels

**Prep time: 15 minutes | Cook time: 6 to 11 minutes | Serves 6**

- 3 tablespoons finely chopped onion
- 2 garlic cloves, minced
- 2 tablespoons grated carrot
- 1 teaspoon olive oil
- 3 tablespoons frozen baby peas, thawed
- 2 tablespoons fat-free soft white cheese, at room temperature
- 6 sheets frozen filo pastry, thawed
- Olive oil spray, for coating the dough

1. In a baking pan, combine the onion, garlic, carrot, and olive oil. Place the pan into Zone 1 and air fry at 200°C for 2 to 4 minutes, or until the vegetables are crisp-tender. Transfer the cooked vegetables to a bowl.
2. Stir the peas and soft white cheese into the vegetable mixture and let it cool while preparing the filo dough. Lay one sheet of filo dough on a work surface and lightly spray with olive oil spray. Top with another sheet of filo. Repeat with the remaining 4 sheets to create 3 stacks, each with 2 layers.
3. Cut each filo stack lengthwise into 4 strips, creating a total of 12 strips. Place about 2 teaspoons of the vegetable filling near the bottom of each strip. Fold one corner over the filling to form a triangle, then continue folding the strip over itself in a triangular shape, like folding a flag. Seal the edge with a dab of water to secure the triangle.
4. Place half of the triangles into Zone 1 and the other half into Zone 2. Air fry at 200°C for 4 to 7 minutes, or until the triangles are crisp and golden brown.
5. Serve the filo vegetable triangles warm, and enjoy their flaky, savory goodness!

## Sweet Churro Nuggets

### Prep time: 5 minutes | Cook time: 6 minutes | Makes 36 bites

- Oil, for spraying
- 1 (500 g) package frozen puffed pastry, thawed
- 180 g caster sugar
- 1 tablespoon ground cinnamon
- 90 g icing sugar
- 1 tablespoon milk

1. Preheat Zone 1 and Zone 2 to 200°C. Line both baskets with parchment paper and spray lightly with oil to prevent sticking.
2. Unfold the puff pastry onto a clean work surface. Using a sharp knife, cut the dough into 36 bite-size pieces.
3. Divide the dough pieces evenly between Zone 1 and Zone 2, arranging them in a single layer without touching or overlapping.
4. Select the MATCH button to sync both zones, set the temperature to 200°C, and set the time for 3 minutes. Press START/PAUSE to begin.
5. After 3 minutes, open the baskets, flip the dough pieces, and continue cooking for another 3 minutes, or until the bites are puffed and golden.
6. While the bites cook, prepare the coatings. In a small bowl, mix the caster sugar and cinnamon until evenly combined. In another bowl, whisk together the icing sugar and milk to create a smooth dipping glaze.
7. Once the bites are cooked, remove them from the air fryer and immediately dredge them in the cinnamon-sugar mixture until evenly coated.
8. Serve the warm cinnamon-sugar puff bites with the icing glaze on the side for dipping. Enjoy this delightful treat!

## Grilled Steak and Veggie Skewers

### Prep time: 15 minutes | Cook time: 5 to 7 minutes | Serves 4

- 2 tablespoons balsamic vinegar
- 2 teaspoons olive oil
- ½ teaspoon dried marjoram
- ⅛ teaspoon ground black pepper
- 340 g silverside, cut into 1-inch pieces
- 1 red pepper, sliced
- 16 button mushrooms
- 235 g cherry tomatoes

1. In a medium bowl, mix the balsamic vinegar, olive oil, marjoram, and black pepper until well combined. Add the steak pieces and toss to coat evenly. Let the steak marinate at room temperature for 10 minutes to absorb the flavors.
2. While the steak marinates, prepare 8 bamboo or metal skewers that fit in the Ninja Double Stack Air Fryer. Thread the beef, red pepper, mushrooms, and tomatoes alternately onto each skewer.
3. Preheat Zone 1 and Zone 2 of the air fryer to 200°C. Use the MATCH button to synchronize both zones, then press START/PAUSE to begin preheating.
4. Place 4 skewers in Zone 1 and 4 skewers in Zone 2, arranging them in a single layer. Air fry for 5 to 7 minutes. Check for doneness by ensuring the beef is browned and registers at least 64°C on a meat thermometer.
5. Once cooking is complete, carefully remove the skewers from the baskets. Serve immediately while warm and enjoy these flavorful kebabs!

## Butter Steak Tips with Potatoes

### Prep time: 10 minutes | Cook time: 20 minutes | Serves 4

- Oil, for spraying
- 227 g baby potatoes, cut in half
- ½ teaspoon salt
- 450 g steak, cut into ½-inch pieces
- 1 teaspoon Worcester sauce
- 1 teaspoon garlic powder
- ½ teaspoon salt
- ½ teaspoon ground black pepper

1. Line Zone 1 and Zone 2 of the Ninja Double Stack Air Fryer with parchment paper and lightly spray with oil to prevent sticking.
2. In a microwave-safe bowl, combine the potatoes and salt. Add about ½ inch of water, cover lightly, and microwave for 7 minutes or until the potatoes are nearly tender. Drain well and set aside.
3. In a large mixing bowl, gently toss the steak, potatoes, Worcestershire sauce, garlic, salt, and black pepper until evenly coated. Divide the mixture equally between Zone 1 and Zone 2.
4. Preheat both zones to 200°C. Use the MATCH button to sync both zones and press START/PAUSE to begin preheating. Once preheated, spread the steak and potato mixture in an even layer across both baskets.
5. Air fry for 12 to 17 minutes, stirring the mixture in both zones after 5 to 6 minutes to ensure even cooking. Adjust the cooking time based on the thickness of the meat and your preferred level of doneness.
6. Once cooked, remove the baskets from the air fryer and serve the steak and potato mixture immediately while hot. Enjoy this hearty and flavorful dish!

# Sugar-Dusted Beignet Treats

**Prep time: 30 minutes | Cook time: 6 minutes | Makes 9 beignets**

- Oil, for greasing and spraying
- 350 g plain flour, plus more for dusting
- 1½ teaspoons salt
- 1 (2¼ teaspoons) instant yeast
- 235 ml milk
- 2 tablespoons packed light muscovado sugar
- 1 tablespoon unsalted butter
- 1 large egg
- 180 g icing sugar

1. Oil a large bowl and set aside. In a small bowl, combine the flour, salt, and yeast, mixing until evenly blended. Heat the milk in a microwave-safe measuring cup in 1-minute intervals until it reaches a boil.
2. In another large bowl, mix the brown sugar and butter. Pour in the hot milk, whisking until the sugar dissolves. Let the mixture cool to room temperature.
3. Once cooled, whisk the egg into the milk mixture, then fold in the flour mixture until a dough forms. Transfer the dough to a lightly floured work surface and knead for 3 to 5 minutes until smooth and elastic.
4. Place the kneaded dough into the oiled bowl, cover with a clean kitchen towel, and let it rise in a warm place for about 1 hour, or until it has doubled in size.
5. Roll out the dough on a lightly floured work surface to about ¼ inch thickness. Cut into 3-inch squares and place them on a lightly floured baking sheet. Cover the squares loosely with a kitchen towel and let them rise again for about 30 minutes, or until doubled in size.
6. Line Zone 1 and Zone 2 with parchment paper and spray lightly with oil. Arrange half the dough squares in Zone 1 and the other half in Zone 2, ensuring they are evenly spaced. Spray the tops lightly with oil.
7. Select the MATCH button to sync both zones. Set the temperature to 200°C and the time to 3 minutes. Press START/PAUSE to begin.
8. After 3 minutes, open the baskets, flip the dough squares, spray them with oil, and resume cooking for another 3 minutes. The squares are done when they are golden and crispy.
9. Remove the cooked dough squares and dust them generously with icing sugar before serving. Enjoy these light, crispy treats warm!

# Chapter 3
# Fast and Easy Everyday Favourites

# Chapter 3 Fast and Easy Everyday Favourites

## Grilled Beef Bratwursts

**Prep time: 5 minutes | Cook time: 15 minutes | Serves 4**

- 4 (85 g) beef bratwursts

1. Preheat Zone 1 and Zone 2 to 190°C.
2. Place the beef bratwursts evenly in Zone 1 and Zone 2 baskets. Use the MATCH button to synchronize both zones, then press START/PAUSE to begin cooking.
3. Air fry the bratwursts for 15 minutes, turning them once halfway through to ensure even browning.
4. Once fully cooked and golden, carefully remove the bratwursts from the air fryer. Serve hot and enjoy!

## Crispy Chorizo-Coated Scotch Eggs

**Prep time: 5 minutes | Cook time: 15 to 20 minutes | Makes 4 eggs**

- 450 g Mexican chorizo or other seasoned banger meat
- 4 soft-boiled eggs plus 1 raw egg
- 1 tablespoon water
- 120 ml plain flour
- 235 ml panko breadcrumbs
- Cooking spray

1. Divide the chorizo into 4 equal portions and flatten each into a disc. Place a soft-boiled egg in the center of each disc and gently wrap the chorizo around the egg, ensuring it is completely encased. Place the wrapped eggs on a plate and chill in the refrigerator for at least 30 minutes.
2. Preheat Zone 1 and Zone 2 to 182°C.
3. Beat the raw egg with 1 tablespoon of water in a small bowl. Place the flour on one plate and the panko on another. Take one encased egg at a time and roll it in the flour, ensuring an even coating. Dip it into the beaten egg mixture, then dredge it in the panko, covering it completely. Repeat with the remaining eggs and place them on a plate.
4. Spray the coated eggs with oil and arrange two eggs in Zone 1 and two in Zone 2. Use the MATCH button to sync the zones and press START/PAUSE to begin cooking.
5. Air fry for 10 minutes, then turn the eggs over and spray with oil again. Continue air frying for an additional 5 to 10 minutes, or until the eggs are golden brown and crispy on all sides.
6. Carefully remove the Scotch eggs from both zones and serve immediately. Enjoy these crispy and flavorful chorizo-wrapped delights!

## Crispy Peppery Rice Patties

**Prep time: 10 minutes | Cook time: 8 to 10 minutes | Serves 4**

- 1 (284 g) bag frozen cooked brown rice, thawed
- 1 egg
- 3 tablespoons brown rice flour
- 80 g finely grated carrots
- 80 g minced red pepper
- 2 tablespoons minced fresh basil
- 3 tablespoons grated Parmesan cheese
- 2 teaspoons olive oil

1. Preheat Zone 1 and Zone 2 to 190°C.
2. In a small bowl, mix the thawed rice, egg, and flour until blended. Add the carrots, pepper, basil, and Parmesan cheese, stirring until the mixture is well combined.
3. Divide the mixture into 8 equal portions and shape each into a fritter. Drizzle the fritters lightly with olive oil to enhance crispiness.
4. Place 4 fritters in Zone 1 and the remaining 4 in Zone 2, arranging them in a single layer to ensure even cooking.
5. Air fry the fritters for 8 to 10 minutes, checking halfway through to ensure even browning. The fritters are done when golden brown and cooked through.
6. Remove the fritters from both zones and serve immediately while warm. Enjoy these flavorful and crispy fritters as a snack or side dish!

## Spicy Cheesy Jalapeño Cornbread

**Prep time: 10 minutes | Cook time: 20 minutes | Serves 8**

- 160 ml cornmeal
- 80 ml plain flour
- ¾ teaspoon baking powder
- 2 tablespoons margarine, melted
- ½ teaspoon rock salt
- 1 tablespoon granulated sugar
- 180 ml whole milk
- 1 large egg, beaten
- 1 red chilli, thinly sliced
- 80 ml shredded extra mature Cheddar cheese
- Cooking spray

1. Set the temperature in Zone 1 and Zone 2 to 152°C and begin preheating. Lightly spritz both baskets with cooking spray to ensure easy removal later. Press the MATCH button to synchronize both zones and hit START/PAUSE to initiate preheating.
2. In a large bowl, combine all the ingredients and stir until the mixture is smooth and fully blended. Pour the batter into two evenly sized baking pans, spreading it out evenly.
3. Place one pan into Zone 1 and the other into Zone 2. Use the MATCH button to sync the zones and start baking for 20 minutes.
4. Check the bread by inserting a toothpick into the center. If it comes out clean, the bread is ready.
5. Carefully remove the baking pans from the air fryer and let the bread cool for a few minutes. Slice and serve warm. Enjoy your freshly baked creation!

## Air Fried Purple Potato Rosemary Chips

**Prep time: 10 minutes | Cook time: 9 to 14 minutes | Serves 6**

- 235 ml Greek yoghurt
- 2 chipotle chillies, minced
- 2 tablespoons adobo or chipotle sauce
- 1 teaspoon paprika
- 1 tablespoon lemon juice
- 10 purple fingerling or miniature potatoes
- 1 teaspoon olive oil
- 2 teaspoons minced fresh rosemary leaves
- ⅛ teaspoon cayenne pepper
- ¼ teaspoon coarse sea salt

1. Preheat Zone 1 and Zone 2 to 200°C.
2. In a medium bowl, mix together the yoghurt, minced chillies, adobo sauce, paprika, and lemon juice until well blended. Cover and refrigerate the chipotle sauce while preparing the potatoes.
3. Wash the potatoes thoroughly and pat them dry with paper towels. Slice them lengthwise as thinly as possible using a mandoline, vegetable peeler, or sharp knife for uniform chips.
4. Place the potato slices in a medium bowl, drizzle with olive oil, and toss to coat evenly.
5. Divide the potato slices between Zone 1 and Zone 2, arranging them in a single layer for even cooking. Air fry for 9 to 14 minutes, checking and using tongs to gently rearrange the chips halfway through cooking.
6. When the chips are golden and crispy, remove them from the air fryer. Sprinkle with rosemary, cayenne pepper, and sea salt while still warm.
7. Serve immediately with the chipotle sauce for dipping. Perfectly crispy and flavorful!

## Fresh Beetroot Salad with Zesty Lemon Dressing

**Prep time: 10 minutes | Cook time: 12 to 15 minutes | Serves 4**

- 6 medium red and golden beetroots, peeled and sliced
- 1 teaspoon olive oil
- ¼ teaspoon rock salt

Vinaigrette:
- 2 teaspoons olive oil
- 2 tablespoons chopped fresh chives
- 120 g crumbled feta cheese
- 2 kg mixed greens
- Cooking spray
- Juice of 1 lemon

1. Preheat Zone 1 and Zone 2 to 180°C. Use the MATCH button to synchronize both zones, then press START/PAUSE to begin preheating.
2. In a large bowl, toss the beetroots with olive oil and rock salt, ensuring they are evenly coated.
3. Spray the baskets of Zone 1 and Zone 2 lightly with cooking spray. Divide the beetroots between the two zones, placing them in a single layer for even cooking.
4. Set the temperature in both zones to 180°C and air fry for 12 to 15 minutes. Check for doneness by piercing the beetroots with a fork; they should be tender.
5. While the beetroots cook, prepare the vinaigrette by whisking olive oil, lemon juice, and chives together in a large bowl.
6. Once the beetroots are done, carefully remove them from both zones and immediately toss them in the vinaigrette to coat. Allow them to cool for 5 minutes to absorb the flavors.
7. Add crumbled feta cheese and serve the dressed beetroots over a bed of mixed greens. Enjoy this refreshing and vibrant salad!

# Veggie Spinach and Carrot Rounds

**Prep time: 10 minutes | Cook time: 10 minutes | Serves 4**

- 2 slices toasted bread
- 1 carrot, peeled and grated
- 1 package fresh spinach, blanched and chopped
- ½ onion, chopped
- 1 egg, beaten
- ½ teaspoon garlic powder
- 1 teaspoon minced garlic
- 1 teaspoon salt
- ½ teaspoon black pepper
- 1 tablespoon Engevita yeast flakes
- 1 tablespoon flour

1. Preheat Zone 1 and Zone 2 to 200°C. Select the MATCH button to sync both zones for simultaneous cooking, then press START/PAUSE to begin preheating.
2. In a food processor, pulse the toasted bread until fine breadcrumbs form. Transfer the breadcrumbs into a shallow dish or bowl.
3. In a separate bowl, combine the remaining ingredients and mix until well incorporated. Use your hands to shape the mixture into small, evenly sized balls.
4. Roll each ball in the breadcrumbs, coating them thoroughly on all sides. Place half of the coated balls in Zone 1 and the other half in Zone 2. Arrange them in a single layer for optimal airflow.
5. Select the MATCH button to synchronize the zones, set the temperature to 200°C, and the time to 10 minutes. Press START/PAUSE to initiate cooking.
6. After 5 minutes, pause the air fryer and gently shake the baskets to ensure even browning. Press START/PAUSE to resume cooking for the remaining time.
7. When the timer ends, carefully remove the balls from both zones using tongs. Serve immediately while hot and crispy. Enjoy these perfectly cooked bites!

# Air Fried Broccoli Bites

**Prep time: 5 minutes | Cook time: 6 minutes | Serves 1**

- 4 egg yolks
- 60 g melted butter
- 240 g coconut flour
- Salt and pepper, to taste
- 475 g broccoli florets

1. Preheat Zone 1 to 200°C. In a bowl, whisk together the egg yolks and melted butter until well combined.
2. Add the coconut flour, salt, and pepper to the bowl, stirring thoroughly to create a smooth batter.
3. Dip each broccoli floret into the batter, ensuring they are evenly coated, and place them in the basket of Zone 1 in a single layer.
4. Air fry for 6 minutes, working in batches if necessary to avoid overcrowding.
5. Carefully remove the crispy broccoli florets from Zone 1 and serve immediately while hot. Enjoy this simple and delicious single-serving dish!

## Baked Halloumi with Fresh Greek Topping

**Prep time: 15 minutes | Cook time: 6 minutes | Serves 4**

Salsa:
- 1 small shallot, finely diced
- 3 garlic cloves, minced
- 2 tablespoons fresh lemon juice
- 2 tablespoons extra-virgin olive oil
- 1 teaspoon freshly cracked black pepper
- Pinch of rock salt
- 120 ml finely diced English cucumber
- 1 plum tomato, deseeded and finely diced
- 2 teaspoons chopped fresh parsley
- 1 teaspoon snipped fresh dill
- 1 teaspoon snipped fresh oregano

Cheese:
- 227 g Halloumi cheese, sliced into ½-inch-thick pieces
- 1 tablespoon extra-virgin olive oil

1. Preheat Zone 1 and Zone 2 to 192°C. Use the MATCH button to sync both zones, then press START/PAUSE to begin preheating.
2. Prepare the salsa in a medium bowl by combining the shallot, garlic, lemon juice, olive oil, pepper, and salt. Add the cucumber, tomato, parsley, dill, and oregano. Toss gently to mix and set aside to allow the flavors to meld.
3. In a separate medium bowl, place the cheese slices and drizzle with olive oil. Toss gently to ensure the cheese is evenly coated.
4. Arrange half of the cheese slices in Zone 1 and the other half in Zone 2, laying them in a single layer for even cooking. Select MATCH to ensure synchronized cooking, then set the time for 6 minutes and press START/PAUSE to bake the cheese until warm and slightly golden.
5. Once cooking is complete, carefully remove the cheese from both zones and divide among four serving plates.
6. Top the warm cheese slices with the prepared salsa and serve immediately.

## Air Fried Butternut Marrow Topped with Hazelnuts

**Prep time: 10 minutes | Cook time: 20 minutes | Makes 700 ml**

- 2 tablespoons whole hazelnuts
- 700 g butternut marrow, peeled, deseeded, and cubed
- ¼ teaspoon rock salt
- ¼ teaspoon freshly ground black pepper
- 2 teaspoons olive oil
- Cooking spray

1. Preheat Zone 1 and Zone 2 to 150°C.
2. Lightly spritz the baskets with cooking spray. Spread the hazelnuts evenly across Zone 1 and Zone 2 and air fry for 3 minutes, or until softened and fragrant.
3. Remove the hazelnuts from the baskets, roughly chop them, and transfer to a small bowl. Set aside for later use.
4. Increase the temperature in Zone 1 and Zone 2 to 180°C. In a large bowl, place the butternut marrow, sprinkle with salt and pepper, and drizzle with olive oil. Toss well to coat evenly.
5. Transfer the seasoned marrow to the baskets of Zone 1 and Zone 2, arranging them in a single layer for even cooking.
6. Air fry for 20 minutes, shaking the baskets halfway through the cooking time to ensure even frying.
7. Once the marrow is tender and golden, remove it from the baskets and transfer to a serving plate. Sprinkle with the chopped hazelnuts and serve immediately. Simple and delicious!

# Chapter 4

## Poultry

# Chapter 4 Poultry

## Teriyaki Chicken Legs

**Prep time: 12 minutes | Cook time: 18 to 20 minutes | Serves 2**

- 4 tablespoons teriyaki sauce
- 1 tablespoon orange juice
- 1 teaspoon smoked paprika
- 4 chicken legs
- Cooking spray

1. Mix the teriyaki sauce, orange juice, and smoked paprika in a small bowl. Generously brush the mixture over all sides of the chicken legs, ensuring they are well coated.
2. Lightly spray the baskets of Zone 1 and Zone 2 with nonstick cooking spray. Divide the chicken legs evenly between the two zones, placing them in a single layer for even cooking. Preheat the air fryer to 180°C by setting the temperature for both zones and pressing START/PAUSE.
3. Air fry the chicken legs for 6 minutes. Open the baskets, turn the chicken legs, and baste them with the remaining sauce. Resume cooking for another 6 minutes.
4. Turn the chicken legs one last time, brush them again with the sauce, and continue air frying for 6 to 8 minutes, or until the juices run clear and the internal temperature reaches 74°C.
5. Remove the chicken legs from the air fryer and serve immediately. Enjoy this delicious and easy meal!

## Crispy Dill Chicken Strips

**Prep time: 30 minutes | Cook time: 10 minutes | Serves 4**

- 2 whole boneless, skinless chicken breasts (about 450 g each), halved lengthwise
- 230 ml Italian dressing
- 110 g finely crushed crisps
- 1 tablespoon dried dill
- 1 tablespoon garlic powder
- 1 large egg, beaten
- 1 to 2 tablespoons oil

1. Place the chicken and Italian dressing in a large resealable bag, ensuring the chicken is evenly coated. Seal the bag and refrigerate for at least 1 hour to marinate.
2. In a shallow dish, combine the crushed potato chips, dill, and garlic powder. In a separate shallow dish, pour the beaten egg and set it aside.
3. Remove the chicken from the marinade and let any excess drip off. Dip each piece into the egg, making sure it is fully coated, then roll it in the potato chip mixture, pressing gently to adhere.
4. Preheat Zone 1 and Zone 2 to 170°C. Line each air fryer basket with parchment paper to prevent sticking and for easy cleanup.
5. Divide the coated chicken evenly between Zone 1 and Zone 2. Lightly spritz the chicken with cooking oil to enhance crispiness.
6. Press the MATCH button to synchronize cooking in both zones and set the timer for 5 minutes. Once the time is up, open both zones, flip the chicken, spritz with oil again, and cook for an additional 5 minutes.
7. When done, check that the chicken is golden brown on the outside and has an internal temperature of 74°C to ensure it is fully cooked.

## Turkey and Cranberry Quesadillas

**Prep time: 7 minutes | Cook time: 4 to 8 minutes | Serves 4**

- 6 low-sodium whole-wheat tortillas
- 75 g shredded low-sodium low-fat Swiss cheese
- 105 g shredded cooked low-sodium turkey breast
- 2 tablespoons cranberry sauce
- 2 tablespoons dried cranberries
- ½ teaspoon dried basil
- Olive oil spray, for spraying the tortillas

1. Preheat Zone 1 and Zone 2 to 200°C.
2. Lay 3 tortillas flat on a work surface. Evenly distribute the Swiss cheese, turkey, cranberry sauce, and dried cranberries among the tortillas. Sprinkle each with basil, then top with the remaining tortillas to form quesadillas.
3. Spray both sides of the tortillas with olive oil spray to ensure crispiness.
4. Place two quesadillas in Zone 1 and the other quesadilla in Zone 2, arranging them in a single layer. Press the AIR FRY button, set the temperature to 200°C, and press the MATCH button to synchronize cooking in both zones.
5. Air fry for 4 to 8 minutes, flipping the quesadillas halfway through, until they are crisp and the cheese is fully melted.
6. Once done, remove the quesadillas from the air fryer and let them cool slightly. Cut each quesadilla into quarters and serve warm. Enjoy the perfect combination of savory and sweet flavors!

## Coconut Chicken Wings with Mango Sauce

**Prep time: 15 minutes | Cook time: 20 minutes | Serves 4**

- 16 chicken drumettes (party wings)
- 60 ml full-fat coconut milk
- 1 tablespoon sriracha
- 1 teaspoon onion powder
- 1 teaspoon garlic powder
- Salt and freshly ground black pepper, to taste
- 25 g shredded unsweetened coconut
- 30 g plain flour
- Cooking oil spray
- 165 g mango, cut into ½-inch chunks
- 15 g fresh coriander, chopped
- 25 g red onion, chopped
- 2 garlic cloves, minced
- Juice of ½ lime

1. Place the drumettes in a resealable plastic bag. In a small bowl, whisk together the coconut milk and sriracha until smooth. Pour the mixture over the drumettes in the bag. Sprinkle the chicken with onion powder, garlic powder, salt, and pepper. Seal the bag and shake thoroughly to coat the chicken evenly with the seasonings and marinade. Marinate in the refrigerator for at least 30 minutes or, for best results, overnight.
2. As the drumettes finish marinating, combine the desiccated coconut and flour in a large bowl. Mix well. Remove the drumettes from the bag and dip each one into the coconut-flour mixture, pressing the coating onto the chicken with your hands to ensure it adheres.
3. Preheat Zone 1 and Zone 2 to 200°C. Select the MATCH button to sync both zones and press START/PAUSE to begin preheating.
4. Once preheated, spray the crisper plates and baskets in Zone 1 and Zone 2 with cooking oil. Arrange half of the drumettes in each zone, stacking them if necessary. Spray the drumettes with cooking oil, ensuring even coverage, including any bottom layers.
5. Select the MATCH button to synchronize the zones, set the temperature to 200°C, and the time to 20 minutes. Press START/PAUSE to begin cooking.
6. After 5 minutes, remove the baskets and shake them to redistribute the chicken for even cooking. Reinsert the baskets and repeat this step every 5 minutes, ensuring the chicken cooks evenly. Use a food thermometer to confirm that the internal temperature of the drumettes reaches 76°C.
7. Once cooking is complete, remove the drumettes from both zones and let them cool for 5 minutes.
8. While the chicken cooks and cools, prepare the salsa. In a small bowl, combine the mango, coriander, red onion, garlic, and lime juice. Stir until fully mixed.

## Crisp Paprika Chicken Drumsticks

**Prep time: 5 minutes | Cook time: 22 minutes | Serves 2**

- 2 teaspoons paprika
- 1 teaspoon packed brown sugar
- 1 teaspoon garlic powder
- ½ teaspoon dry mustard
- ½ teaspoon salt
- Pinch pepper
- 4 (140 g) chicken drumsticks, trimmed
- 1 teaspoon vegetable oil
- 1 scallion, green part only, sliced thin on bias

1. Preheat Zone 1 and Zone 2 to 200°C.
2. In a bowl, mix paprika, sugar, garlic powder, mustard, salt, and pepper. Pat the drumsticks dry with paper towels and poke 10 to 15 holes in the skin of each drumstick using a metal skewer. Rub the drumsticks with oil and coat evenly with the spice mixture.
3. Divide the drumsticks evenly between Zone 1 and Zone 2, spacing them apart and alternating ends for even cooking. Select AIR FRY, set the temperature to 200°C, and press MATCH to synchronize zones. Cook for 22 to 25 minutes, flipping halfway through, until the chicken is crispy and the internal temperature reaches 90°C.
4. Transfer the drumsticks to a serving platter, tent loosely with foil, and let rest for 5 minutes. Sprinkle with scallions and serve.

## Lemon-Basil Turkey Breasts

**Prep time: 30 minutes | Cook time: 58 minutes | Serves 4**

- 2 tablespoons olive oil
- 900 g turkey breasts, bone-in, skin-on
- Coarse sea salt and ground black pepper, to taste
- 1 teaspoon fresh basil leaves, chopped
- 2 tablespoons lemon zest, grated

1. Rub olive oil evenly over all sides of the turkey breasts. Sprinkle with salt, pepper, basil, and lemon zest for seasoning.
2. Place the turkey breasts skin-side up in Zone 1 and Zone 2 on parchment-lined baskets.
3. Select AIR FRY, set the temperature to 170°C, and press MATCH to synchronize both zones. Cook for 30 minutes, then turn the turkey breasts over and cook for an additional 28 minutes.
4. Once done, serve with lemon wedges if desired. Enjoy your flavorful turkey!

## Chicken and Gruyère Cordon Bleu

**Prep time: 15 minutes | Cook time: 15 minutes | Serves 4**

- 4 chicken breast filets
- 75 g chopped gammon
- 75 g grated Swiss cheese, or Gruyère cheese
- 15 g plain flour
- Pinch salt
- Freshly ground black pepper, to taste
- ½ teaspoon dried marjoram
- 1 egg
- 60 g panko bread crumbs
- Olive oil spray

1. Place the chicken breast filets on a work surface and press gently to flatten slightly without tearing.
2. Mix the gammon and cheese in a small bowl. Divide the mixture evenly among the filets, then wrap the chicken around the filling and secure with toothpicks.
3. Combine the flour, salt, pepper, and marjoram in a shallow bowl. Beat the egg in another bowl, and spread the panko on a plate.
4. Coat each chicken roll in the flour mixture, dip in the egg, and dredge in the panko, pressing to adhere the coating.
5. Preheat Zone 1 and Zone 2 by selecting BAKE, setting the temperature to 190ºC, and the time to 3 minutes. Press START/PAUSE to begin.
6. Spray the crisper plates in both zones with olive oil. Place the chicken rolls in a single layer in Zone 1 and Zone 2. Spray the tops with olive oil.
7. Select BAKE, set the temperature to 190ºC, and the time to 15 minutes. Press MATCH to synchronize zones, then press START/PAUSE.
8. Flip the rolls halfway through if desired. When done, ensure the chicken is fully cooked to 76ºC. Remove toothpicks before serving.
9. Serve warm and enjoy the crispy, cheesy chicken rolls.

## Buttermilk Breaded Chicken

**Prep time: 7 minutes | Cook time: 20 to 25 minutes | Serves 4**

- 125 g plain flour
- 2 teaspoons paprika
- Pinch salt
- Freshly ground black pepper, to taste
- 80 ml buttermilk
- 2 eggs
- 2 tablespoons extra-virgin olive oil
- 185 g bread crumbs
- 6 chicken pieces, drumsticks, breasts, and thighs, patted dry
- Cooking oil spray

1. Mix the flour, paprika, salt, and pepper in a shallow bowl.
2. In another bowl, beat the buttermilk and eggs until smooth.
3. Combine olive oil and breadcrumbs in a third bowl, mixing well.
4. Coat the chicken in the flour mixture, dip into the egg mixture, and press into the breadcrumbs, ensuring a firm coating.
5. Preheat Zone 1 and Zone 2 by selecting AIR FRY, setting the temperature to 190ºC, and the time to 3 minutes. Press START/PAUSE to begin.
6. Once preheated, spray the crisper plates with cooking oil. Divide the chicken between Zone 1 and Zone 2, placing them in a single layer.
7. Select AIR FRY, set the temperature to 190ºC, and the time to 25 minutes. Press MATCH to synchronize both zones, then press START/PAUSE to begin cooking.
8. After 10 minutes, flip the chicken and continue cooking. Check the chicken after another 10 minutes. If it is golden brown and a thermometer reads 76ºC, it is done. If needed, cook for an additional 5 minutes.
9. Let the chicken rest for 5 minutes before serving. Enjoy the crispy and flavorful result!

## Broccoli Cheese Chicken

**Prep time: 15 minutes | Cook time: 25 minutes | Serves 4**

- 1 tablespoon avocado oil
- 15 g chopped onion
- 35 g finely chopped broccoli
- 115 g cream cheese, at room temperature
- 60 g Cheddar cheese, shredded
- 1 teaspoon garlic powder
- ½ teaspoon sea salt, plus additional for seasoning, divided
- ¼ freshly ground black pepper, plus additional for seasoning, divided
- 900 g boneless, skinless chicken breasts
- 1 teaspoon smoked paprika

1. Heat a frying pan over medium-high heat and add avocado oil. Cook the onion and broccoli for 5 to 8 minutes, stirring occasionally, until the onion is tender.
2. Transfer the mixture to a bowl and stir in cream cheese, Cheddar cheese, and garlic powder. Season with salt and pepper to taste.
3. Cut a pocket into each chicken breast using a sharp knife, keeping the knife parallel to the breast. Fill each pocket with the broccoli mixture and secure with toothpicks.
4. Mix paprika, ½ teaspoon salt, and ¼ teaspoon pepper in a small dish. Sprinkle the seasoning evenly over the chicken.
5. Preheat Zone 1 and Zone 2 to 200ºC. Divide the stuffed chicken evenly between both zones, placing them in a single layer.
6. Select AIR FRY, set the temperature to 200ºC, and cook for 14 to 16 minutes, pressing MATCH to synchronize zones. Check that an instant-read thermometer inserted into the chicken reads 70ºC.
7. Transfer the chicken to a plate and tent with foil. Let rest for 5 to 10 minutes before serving to allow the juices to settle. Enjoy!

# Garlic Soy Chicken Thighs & Chicken Paillard

**Prep time: 10 minutes | Cook time: 30 minutes**

### Garlic Soy Chicken Thighs | Serves 1 to 2

- 2 tablespoons chicken stock
- 2 tablespoons reduced-sodium soy sauce
- 1½ tablespoons sugar
- 4 garlic cloves, smashed and peeled
- 2 large spring onions, cut into 2- to 3-inch batons, plus more, thinly sliced, for garnish
- 2 bone-in, skin-on chicken thighs (198 to 225 g each)

### Chicken Paillard | Serves 1 to 2

- 2 large eggs, room temperature
- 1 tablespoon water
- 20 g powdered Parmesan cheese or pork dust
- 2 teaspoons dried thyme

Lemon Butter Sauce:
- 2 tablespoons unsalted butter, melted
- 2 teaspoons lemon juice
- ¼ teaspoon finely chopped fresh thyme leaves, plus more for garnish
- ⅛ teaspoon fine sea salt
- Lemon slices, for serving
- 1 teaspoon ground black pepper
- 2 (140 g) boneless, skinless chicken breasts, pounded to ½ inch thick

### For Garlic Soy Chicken Thighs:

1. Preheat Zone 1 to 190°C.
2. In a metal cake pan that fits the air fryer basket, mix the chicken stock, soy sauce, and sugar, stirring until the sugar dissolves completely. Add the garlic cloves, spring onions, and chicken thighs, turning the thighs to coat them in the marinade. Arrange the thighs skin-side up in the pan.
3. Place the pan into Zone 1 of the air fryer and bake for 30 minutes. After the first 10 minutes, begin flipping the thighs every 5 minutes to ensure even cooking. Let the marinade gradually reduce into a sticky glaze over the chicken.
4. Once the chicken is fully cooked and the glaze has thickened, remove the pan from Zone 1. Confirm the internal temperature of the chicken reaches 76°C to ensure safety.
5. Serve the chicken thighs warm, spooning any remaining glaze over the top and garnishing with additional sliced spring onions. Enjoy!

### For Chicken Paillard:

1. Spray Zone 2 of the Ninja Double Stack Air Fryer basket with avocado oil. Preheat Zone 2 to 200°C.
2. In a shallow dish, beat the eggs thoroughly, then stir in the water until well mixed.
3. In another shallow dish, combine the Parmesan, thyme, and pepper, ensuring the ingredients are evenly blended.
4. Dip each chicken breast into the egg mixture, letting any excess drip off, then coat both sides of the chicken in the Parmesan mixture. Place the coated chicken in Zone 2 of the air fryer basket, leaving space for proper airflow around each piece.
5. Roast the chicken in Zone 2 for 5 minutes. Open the basket, flip the chicken, and cook for an additional 5 minutes, or until the chicken is cooked through and reaches an internal temperature of 76°C.
6. While the chicken cooks, prepare the lemon butter sauce by mixing all the sauce ingredients in a small bowl until smooth and well combined.
7. Plate the chicken once cooked and pour the lemon butter sauce over it. Garnish with chopped fresh thyme and serve with lemon slices for added brightness.
8. Store any leftovers in an airtight container in the refrigerator for up to 4 days. Reheat them in Zone 2 of the preheated 200°C Ninja Double Stack Air Fryer for 5 minutes, or until heated through.

# Classic Whole Chicken

**Prep time: 5 minutes | Cook time: 50 minutes | Serves 4**

- Oil, for spraying
- 1 (1.8 kg) whole chicken, giblets removed
- 1 tablespoon olive oil
- 1 teaspoon paprika
- ½ teaspoon granulated garlic
- ½ teaspoon salt
- ½ teaspoon freshly ground black pepper
- ¼ teaspoon finely chopped fresh parsley, for garnish

1. Line Zone 1 and Zone 2 with parchment paper and spray lightly with oil to prevent sticking.
2. Pat the chicken dry with paper towels and rub it all over with olive oil to ensure an even coating.
3. In a small bowl, mix the paprika, garlic powder, salt, and black pepper. Sprinkle the seasoning mixture evenly over the chicken, coating all sides.
4. Divide the seasoned chicken pieces between Zone 1 and Zone 2, placing them in a single layer with space for proper airflow. Position breast-side down if using whole chicken portions.
5. Select AIR FRY, set the temperature to 180°C, and the time to 30 minutes. Press the MATCH button to synchronize both zones and press START/PAUSE to begin cooking.
6. After 30 minutes, flip the chicken pieces, then continue cooking for another 20 minutes. Ensure the internal temperature reaches 76°C and the juices run clear before removing.
7. Sprinkle the chicken with fresh parsley before serving. Enjoy the perfectly seasoned and crispy chicken!

## Gochujang Chicken Wings

**Prep time: 15 minutes | Cook time: 25 minutes | Serves 4**

Wings:
- 900 g chicken wings
- 1 teaspoon kosher salt
- 1 teaspoon black pepper or gochugaru (Korean red pepper)

Sauce:
- 2 tablespoons gochujang (Korean chilli paste)
- 1 tablespoon mayonnaise
- 1 tablespoon toasted sesame oil
- 1 tablespoon minced fresh ginger
- 1 tablespoon minced garlic
- 1 teaspoon sugar
- 1 teaspoon agave nectar or honey
- For Serving
- 1 teaspoon sesame seeds
- 25 g chopped spring onions

1. Season the wings with salt and pepper, then place them in Zone 1 and Zone 2. Select AIR FRY, set to 200ºC for 20 minutes, and press MATCH to synchronize zones. Flip the wings halfway through cooking.
2. For the sauce, mix the gochujang, mayonnaise, sesame oil, ginger, garlic, sugar, and agave in a small bowl.
3. Near the end of cooking, check the wings with a meat thermometer. Once they reach 70ºC, transfer to a large bowl and toss with half the sauce.
4. Return the wings to Zone 1 and Zone 2. Air fry for 5 more minutes until the sauce glazes the wings.
5. Transfer to a serving platter, sprinkle with sesame seeds and spring onions, and serve with the remaining sauce for dipping.

## Buttermilk-Fried Drumsticks

**Prep time: 10 minutes | Cook time: 25 minutes | Serves 2**

- 1 egg
- 120 g buttermilk
- 45 g self-rising flour
- 45 g seasoned panko bread crumbs
- 1 teaspoon salt
- ¼ teaspoon ground black pepper (to mix into coating)
- 4 chicken drumsticks, skin on
- Oil for misting or cooking spray

1. In a shallow dish, beat the egg and buttermilk together until well combined. In a second shallow dish, mix the flour, panko crumbs, salt, and pepper.
2. Season the chicken legs with additional salt and pepper to taste. Dip each leg into the buttermilk mixture, ensuring it is fully coated, then roll it in the panko mixture. Press the crumbs firmly onto the chicken to help the coating adhere. Lightly mist the coated legs with oil or cooking spray.
3. Preheat Zone 1 and Zone 2 to 180ºC. Spray both baskets lightly with cooking spray to prevent sticking. Arrange the drumsticks in a single layer, dividing them evenly between Zone 1 and Zone 2. If the drumsticks vary in size, place larger ones in one zone and smaller ones in the other for even cooking.
4. Air fry for 10 minutes. Pause the cooking cycle, open the baskets, and turn the drumsticks over. Resume cooking for an additional 10 minutes.
5. After 20 minutes, check the drumsticks for even browning. If any white spots remain, spritz those areas with oil or cooking spray. Continue cooking for an additional 5 minutes, or until the crust is golden brown, the juices run clear, and the internal temperature of the chicken reaches 76ºC.
6. Once fully cooked, remove the drumsticks from both zones and let them cool slightly. Enjoy these crispy, flavorful chicken drumsticks fresh from the air fryer!

## Chicken Breasts with Asparagus, Beans, and Rocket

**Prep time: 20 minutes | Cook time: 25 minutes | Serves 2**

- 160 g canned cannellini beans, rinsed
- 1½ tablespoons red wine vinegar
- 1 garlic clove, minced
- 2 tablespoons extra-virgin olive oil, divided
- Salt and ground black pepper, to taste
- ½ red onion, sliced thinly
- 230 g asparagus, trimmed and cut into 1-inch lengths
- 2 (230 g) boneless, skinless chicken breasts, trimmed
- ¼ teaspoon paprika
- ½ teaspoon ground coriander
- 60 g baby rocket, rinsed and drained

1. Preheat Zone 1 and Zone 2 to 200ºC.
2. Warm the beans in the microwave for 1 minute, then mix them with red wine vinegar, garlic, 1 tablespoon olive oil, ¼ teaspoon salt, and ¼ teaspoon ground black pepper in a bowl.
3. In a separate bowl, toss the onion with ⅛ teaspoon salt, ⅛ teaspoon ground black pepper, and 2 teaspoons olive oil.
4. Place the onion in Zone 1 and air fry for 2 minutes. Add the asparagus to Zone 1 and continue air frying for 8 minutes, shaking the basket halfway through, until tender. Transfer the onion and asparagus to the bowl with the beans and set aside.
5. Toss the chicken breasts with the remaining ingredients, except the baby rocket, in a large bowl.
6. Place the chicken breasts in Zone 2. Select AIR FRY, set to 200ºC, and cook for 14 minutes, flipping halfway through, until the chicken reaches an internal temperature of 76ºC.
7. Remove the chicken and serve with the asparagus, beans, onion, and rocket. Sprinkle with salt and pepper, toss everything together, and enjoy!

## Stuffed Chicken Florentine

**Prep time: 10 minutes | Cook time: 20 minutes | Serves 4**

- 3 tablespoons pine nuts
- 40 g frozen spinach, thawed and squeezed dry
- 75 g ricotta cheese
- 2 tablespoons grated Parmesan cheese
- 3 cloves garlic, minced
- Salt and freshly ground black pepper, to taste
- 4 small boneless, skinless chicken breast halves (about 680 g)
- 8 slices bacon

1. Divide the pine nuts between two small heatproof pans. Place one pan in Zone 1 and the other in Zone 2 of the Ninja Double Stack Air Fryer. Press the AIR FRY button, set the temperature to 200°C, and toast the pine nuts for 2 to 3 minutes, shaking the pans halfway through. Once toasted, transfer the pine nuts to a mixing bowl and continue preheating the air fryer for the chicken.
2. In a large bowl, combine the spinach, ricotta, Parmesan, and garlic. Add salt and pepper to taste, stirring well until the mixture is evenly combined.
3. Use a sharp knife to carefully slice horizontally into each chicken breast, creating a pocket without cutting all the way through. Season both sides of the chicken with salt and pepper.
4. Spoon equal amounts of the spinach mixture into each chicken pocket. Fold the top half of the chicken over the filling, then wrap each chicken breast tightly with 2 slices of bacon to secure the stuffing.
5. Place half of the stuffed chicken breasts in Zone 1 and the other half in Zone 2. Press the ROAST button, set the temperature to 180°C, and press the MATCH button to synchronize cooking in both zones. Roast the chicken for 18 to 20 minutes, flipping halfway through.
6. Check that the bacon is crisp and the chicken reaches an internal temperature of 76°C using a meat thermometer. If necessary, cook for an additional 2 to 3 minutes to ensure doneness.
7. Remove the chicken from both zones and let it rest for 3 to 5 minutes before serving. Serve warm and enjoy the perfectly roasted, stuffed, and bacon-wrapped chicken!

## Piri-Piri Chicken Thighs

**Prep time: 5 minutes | Cook time: 25 minutes | Serves 4**

- 60 ml piri-piri sauce
- 1 tablespoon freshly squeezed lemon juice
- 2 tablespoons brown sugar, divided
- 2 cloves garlic, minced
- 1 tablespoon extra-virgin olive oil
- 4 bone-in, skin-on chicken thighs, each weighing approximately 200 to 230 g
- ½ teaspoon cornflour

1. Prepare the marinade by whisking together the piri-piri sauce, lemon juice, 1 tablespoon of brown sugar, and minced garlic in a small bowl. Slowly drizzle in the olive oil while whisking continuously until the mixture emulsifies. Use a skewer to poke small holes into the chicken thighs, then place them in a shallow glass dish. Pour the marinade over the chicken and turn the pieces to ensure they are thoroughly coated. Cover the dish with plastic wrap and refrigerate for at least 15 minutes or up to 1 hour.
2. Preheat the Ninja Double Stack Air Fryer by selecting MATCH, setting the temperature to 190°C, and pressing START/PAUSE. While the air fryer preheats, remove the chicken thighs from the marinade, reserving the remaining marinade for later use. Place the thighs skin-side down into both Zone 1 and Zone 2 baskets, dividing them evenly to prevent overcrowding. Press START/PAUSE to begin cooking. Air fry the chicken thighs for 15 to 20 minutes, or until the internal temperature of the thickest part reaches 76°C.
3. While the chicken is cooking, whisk the remaining 1 tablespoon of brown sugar and cornflour into the reserved marinade. Microwave the mixture on high for 1 minute, stirring halfway through, until it thickens into a bubbling glaze.
4. When the chicken thighs are cooked, carefully turn them over so the skin side is facing up. Brush each piece generously with the prepared glaze. Return the baskets to the air fryer, select MATCH again, and air fry at 190°C for an additional 2 to 3 minutes, or until the glaze is caramelized and slightly charred in spots.
5. Remove the chicken from the air fryer and transfer to a serving platter.
6. Serve hot, with extra piri-piri sauce on the side if desired.

## Chicken Enchiladas

**Prep time: 10 minutes | Cook time: 8 minutes | Serves 4**

- Oil, for spraying
- 420 g shredded cooked chicken
- 1 package taco seasoning
- 8 flour corn wraps, at room temperature
- 60 g canned black beans, rinsed and drained
- 1 (115 g) tin diced green chilies, drained
- 1 (280 g) tin red or green enchilada sauce
- 235 g shredded Cheddar cheese

1. Line both Zone 1 and Zone 2 of the Ninja Double Stack Air Fryer baskets with parchment paper and spray lightly with oil. This step is essential to prevent the sauce and cheese from dripping through the holes.
2. In a small bowl, combine the chicken and taco seasoning, mixing until the chicken is well-coated.
3. Divide the chicken mixture evenly among the corn wraps. Add black beans and green chilis to each wrap, then carefully roll them up, securing the filling inside.
4. Distribute the enchiladas seam-side down between Zone 1 and Zone 2 baskets, arranging them in a single layer in each basket to allow proper airflow.
5. Spoon enchilada sauce over the enchiladas, using just enough to prevent them from drying out during cooking. Reserve additional sauce for serving. Sprinkle the shredded cheese evenly over the top of the enchiladas.
6. Select the MATCH button to synchronize both zones, set the temperature to 180ºC, and cook for 5 to 8 minutes. The enchiladas are done when heated through and the cheese is melted and bubbling.
7. Once cooked, transfer the enchiladas to plates, placing two enchiladas per serving. Drizzle with extra enchilada sauce, if desired, and serve immediately.

## Sesame Chicken Breast

**Prep time: 10 minutes | Cook time: 18 minutes | Serves 6**

- Oil, for spraying
- 2 (170 g) boneless, skinless chicken breasts, cut into bite-size pieces
- 30 g cornflour plus 1 tablespoon
- 60 ml soy sauce
- 2 tablespoons packed light brown sugar
- 2 tablespoons pineapple juice
- 1 tablespoon black treacle
- ½ teaspoon ground ginger
- 1 tablespoon water
- 2 teaspoons sesame seeds

1. Line Zone 1 and Zone 2 of the Ninja Double Stack Air Fryer baskets with parchment paper and spray lightly with oil to prevent sticking.
2. Place the chicken and 60 g of cornflour in a zip-top plastic bag, seal tightly, and shake until the chicken is evenly coated.
3. Distribute the coated chicken evenly between Zone 1 and Zone 2 in a single layer, spraying liberally with oil. Adjust the quantities if needed to avoid overcrowding and ensure proper airflow.
4. Set the air fryer temperature to 200ºC. Press the MATCH button to synchronize both zones and cook for 9 minutes. Flip the chicken, spray with more oil, and continue cooking for an additional 8 to 9 minutes, or until the internal temperature reaches 76ºC.
5. While the chicken is cooking, prepare the sauce. In a small saucepan, combine the soy sauce, brown sugar, pineapple juice, black treacle, and ginger over medium heat. Stir frequently until the brown sugar dissolves completely.
6. In a small bowl, mix the water and the remaining 1 tablespoon of cornflour until smooth. Gradually pour this mixture into the saucepan with the soy sauce mixture, stirring constantly.
7. Bring the sauce to a boil, continuing to stir until it thickens. Once thickened, remove the saucepan from the heat.
8. When the chicken is finished cooking, transfer it to a large bowl. Pour the sauce over the chicken and toss until evenly coated. Garnish with sesame seeds and serve immediately.

# Chicken Pesto Parmigiana

**Prep time: 10 minutes | Cook time: 23 minutes | Serves 4**

- 2 large eggs
- 1 tablespoon water
- Fine sea salt and ground black pepper, to taste
- 45 g powdered Parmesan cheese
- 2 teaspoons Italian seasoning
- 4 (140 g) boneless, skinless chicken breasts or thighs, pounded to ¼ inch thick
- 65 g pesto
- 115 g shredded Mozzarella cheese
- Finely chopped fresh basil, for garnish (optional)
- Grape tomatoes, halved, for serving (optional)

1. Spray Zone 1 and Zone 2 with avocado oil and preheat both to 200°C.
2. In a shallow dish, whisk together the eggs, water, and a pinch of salt and pepper. In another shallow dish, combine Parmesan and Italian seasoning.
3. Season the chicken breasts on both sides with salt and pepper. Dip each breast in the egg mixture, allowing excess to drip off, then coat both sides in the Parmesan mixture. Spray each breast with avocado oil.
4. Divide the chicken evenly between Zone 1 and Zone 2, placing them in a single layer. Select AIR FRY, set to 200°C, and cook for 20 minutes. Flip halfway through cooking to ensure even browning, and check that the internal temperature reaches 76°C.
5. Dollop ¼ of the pesto on each chicken breast and top with Mozzarella. Return to the air fryer and cook for an additional 3 minutes, or until the cheese is melted.
6. Garnish with fresh basil and serve with halved grape tomatoes, if desired. Store leftovers in an airtight container in the refrigerator for up to 4 days. Reheat at 200°C in the air fryer for 5 minutes, or until warmed through.

# French Garlic Chicken

**Prep time: 30 minutes | Cook time: 27 minutes | Serves 4**

- 2 tablespoon extra-virgin olive oil
- 1 tablespoon Dijon mustard
- 1 tablespoon apple cider vinegar
- 3 cloves garlic, minced
- 2 teaspoons herbes de Provence
- ½ teaspoon kosher salt
- 1 teaspoon black pepper
- 450 g boneless, skinless chicken thighs, halved crosswise
- 2 tablespoons butter
- 8 cloves garlic, chopped
- 60 g heavy whipping cream

1. In a small bowl, combine the olive oil, mustard, vinegar, minced garlic, herbes de Provence, salt, and pepper. Whisk the mixture until emulsified to create a smooth marinade.
2. Pierce the chicken breasts all over with a fork to help the marinade penetrate deeply. Place the chicken in a resealable plastic bag, pour the marinade over, and seal the bag. Massage to coat the chicken evenly. Marinate at room temperature for 30 minutes or refrigerate for up to 24 hours.
3. Preheat Zone 1 to 200°C. In a baking pan that fits Zone 1, add the butter and half of the chopped garlic. Place the pan in Zone 1 and cook for 5 minutes, or until the butter melts and the garlic sizzles.
4. Preheat Zone 2 to 200°C. Add the chicken breasts along with the marinade to Zone 2 in a single layer. Lower the temperature to 180°C and cook for 15 minutes, flipping the chicken halfway through. Ensure the chicken reaches an internal temperature of 76°C using a meat thermometer.
5. While Zone 2 cooks the chicken, add the cream to the garlic butter in the pan in Zone 1. Stir to combine the cream with the butter, garlic, and any cooking juices. Set Zone 1 to 180°C and cook for 7 minutes, allowing the sauce to thicken slightly.
6. Once both zones finish cooking, plate the chicken and pour the creamy garlic butter sauce from Zone 1 over the top. Serve warm and enjoy the rich, flavorful dish.

## Buffalo Crispy Chicken Strips

**Prep time: 15 minutes | Cook time: 13 to 17 minutes per batch | Serves 4**

- 45 g plain flour
- 2 eggs
- 2 tablespoons water
- 60 g seasoned panko bread crumbs
- 2 teaspoons granulated garlic
- 1 teaspoon salt
- 1 teaspoon freshly ground black pepper
- 16 chicken breast strips, or 3 large boneless, skinless chicken breasts, cut into 1-inch strips
- Olive oil spray
- 60 ml Buffalo sauce, plus more as needed

1. Place the flour in a small bowl. In another small bowl, whisk together the eggs and water. In a third bowl, mix the panko, granulated garlic, salt, and pepper until evenly combined.
2. Dip each chicken strip first in the flour, then in the egg mixture, and finally in the panko mixture. Press the panko crumbs onto the chicken strips with your fingers to ensure an even coating.
3. Preheat Zone 1 and Zone 2 to 190°C. Insert parchment liners into the baskets to prevent sticking. Arrange the chicken strips in a single layer in both zones. If needed, use a wire rack for a second layer in either zone to prevent stacking. Spray the tops of the chicken with olive oil.
4. Set both zones to AIR FRY at 190°C for 17 minutes. Press the MATCH button to synchronize the cooking time and temperature, then press START/PAUSE to begin cooking.
5. After 10 to 12 minutes, pause the cooking cycle. Open the baskets, flip the chicken strips, and spray them again with olive oil. Reinsert the baskets and resume cooking.
6. When the cooking is complete, check that the chicken strips are golden brown and crispy. Use a food thermometer to ensure they have reached an internal temperature of 76°C.
7. Transfer the cooked chicken strips to a large bowl. Drizzle Buffalo sauce over the top, toss to coat evenly, and serve while hot. Repeat the process for any remaining chicken strips. Enjoy the perfect balance of crunch and spice!

## Peachy Chicken Chunks with Cherries

**Prep time: 8 minutes | Cook time: 14 to 16 minutes | Serves 4**

- 100 g peach preserves
- 1 teaspoon ground rosemary
- ½ teaspoon black pepper
- ½ teaspoon salt
- ½ teaspoon marjoram
- 1 teaspoon light olive oil
- 450 g boneless chicken breasts, cut in 1½-inch chunks
- Oil for misting or cooking spray
- 1 (280 g) package frozen unsweetened dark cherries, thawed and drained

1. In a medium bowl, combine the peach preserves, rosemary, pepper, salt, marjoram, and olive oil. Mix well until the ingredients are evenly blended.
2. Add the chicken chunks to the bowl and toss thoroughly, ensuring each piece is well coated with the preserve mixture.
3. Preheat Zone 1 and Zone 2 to 200°C. Spray both baskets with oil or cooking spray to prevent sticking.
4. Divide the coated chicken chunks evenly between Zone 1 and Zone 2, spreading them in a single layer for even cooking.
5. Press the MATCH button to synchronize both zones and air fry for 7 minutes. Open the baskets, stir the chicken chunks, and continue cooking for an additional 6 to 8 minutes, or until the chicken is fully cooked and its juices run clear.
6. Once the chicken is cooked through, scatter the cherries evenly over the chicken in both zones. Cook for 1 more minute to warm the cherries.
7. Remove the chicken and cherries from the air fryer and serve warm. Enjoy the sweet and savory flavors!

# Golden Tenders

**Prep time: 10 minutes | Cook time: 15 minutes | Serves 4**

- 60 g panko bread crumbs
- 1 tablespoon paprika
- ½ teaspoon salt
- ¼ teaspoon freshly ground black pepper
- 16 chicken tenders
- 115 g mayonnaise
- Olive oil spray

1. In a medium bowl, mix together the panko, paprika, salt, and pepper until well combined.
2. In a large bowl, toss the chicken tenders with mayonnaise, ensuring they are evenly coated. Transfer the coated chicken to the bowl of seasoned panko and dredge each piece thoroughly. Use your fingers to press the coating firmly onto the chicken.
3. Preheat both Zone 1 and Zone 2 by pressing the AIR FRY button, setting the temperature to 180ºC, and the time to 3 minutes. Press START/PAUSE to begin preheating.
4. Once preheated, line each basket with parchment paper. Divide the coated chicken tenders evenly between Zone 1 and Zone 2, arranging them in a single layer. Spray the chicken tenders with olive oil to enhance crispiness.
5. Select the AIR FRY button again, set the temperature to 180ºC, and the time to 15 minutes. Press the MATCH button to synchronize both zones, then press START/PAUSE to begin cooking.
6. Halfway through cooking, remove both baskets and flip the tenders for even browning. Spray the flipped side with additional olive oil and return the baskets to the unit to resume cooking.
7. When the cooking is complete, the tenders should be golden brown and a food thermometer inserted into the thickest part of the chicken should read 76ºC. If needed, add an extra 1 to 2 minutes of cooking to ensure proper doneness.
8. Remove the chicken tenders from both zones and serve immediately. Enjoy crispy, perfectly browned chicken tenders!

# Korean Honey Wings

**Prep time: 10 minutes | Cook time: 25 minutes per batch | Serves 4**

- 55 g gochujang, or red pepper paste
- 55 g mayonnaise
- 2 tablespoons honey
- 1 tablespoon sesame oil
- 2 teaspoons minced garlic
- 1 tablespoon sugar
- 2 teaspoons ground ginger
- 1.4 kg whole chicken wings
- Olive oil spray
- 1 teaspoon salt
- ½ teaspoon freshly ground black pepper

1. In a large bowl, whisk together the gochujang, mayonnaise, honey, sesame oil, garlic, sugar, and ginger until smooth. Set the sauce aside for later use.
2. Preheat Zone 1 and Zone 2 to 200ºC. Press the MATCH button to synchronize both zones, then press START/PAUSE to begin preheating.
3. Prepare the chicken wings by cutting them in half to separate the drumettes from the flats. Remove and discard the wing tips, or save them for making chicken stock.
4. Once preheated, spray the crisper plates in Zone 1 and Zone 2 with olive oil. Divide the chicken wings evenly between the two zones, arranging them in a single layer. Lightly spray the wings with olive oil and season them with salt and pepper.
5. Set both zones to AIR FRY at 200ºC for 20 minutes and press START/PAUSE to begin cooking. After 10 minutes, pause the air fryer, open the baskets, and flip the wings. Spray with additional olive oil before resuming cooking.
6. Check that the wings are cooked to an internal temperature of 76ºC. Transfer the cooked wings from both zones into the bowl with the prepared sauce and toss them to coat thoroughly.
7. Return the sauced wings to Zone 1 and Zone 2. Air fry at 200ºC for 4 to 6 minutes to glaze the sauce and crisp the chicken. After 3 minutes, check the wings to ensure they are not overcooking.
8. Remove the wings from the air fryer and serve immediately while hot. These sticky, flavorful wings are sure to be a crowd-pleaser!

## Thai Chicken with Cucumber and Chili Salad

**Prep time: 25 minutes | Cook time: 25 minutes | Serves 6**

- 2 (570 g) small chickens, giblets discarded
- 1 tablespoon fish sauce
- 6 tablespoons chopped fresh coriander
- 2 teaspoons lime zest
- 1 teaspoon ground coriander
- 2 garlic cloves, minced
- 2 tablespoons packed light brown sugar
- 2 teaspoons vegetable oil
- Salt and ground black pepper, to taste
- 1 English cucumber, halved lengthwise and sliced thin
- 1 Thai chilli, stemmed, deseeded, and minced
- 2 tablespoons chopped dry-roasted peanuts
- 1 small shallot, sliced thinly
- 1 tablespoon lime juice
- Lime wedges, for serving
- Cooking spray

1 teaspoon of vegetable oil, ½ teaspoon of salt, and ⅛ teaspoon of ground black pepper. Mix well and rub the mixture under the breast and thigh skin of each chicken. Let them sit for 10 minutes to marinate.
3. Preheat Zone 1 and Zone 2 to 200°C. Spritz the baskets with cooking spray.
4. Arrange two marinated chicken halves in Zone 1 and the other two in Zone 2, skin side down. Use the MATCH button to synchronize both zones and press START/PAUSE to begin air frying.
5. Air fry for 15 minutes, then pause the cooking. Open the baskets, gently turn the chickens over, and resume cooking for another 10 minutes, or until the skin is golden brown and the internal temperature reads at least 76°C.
6. While the chickens cook, prepare the salad. In a large bowl, combine all the remaining ingredients except the lime wedges. Sprinkle with salt and black pepper, then toss to mix well.
7. Once the chickens are done, carefully remove them from the air fryer and transfer to a large plate. Serve alongside the salad, squeezing fresh lime wedges over the chickens just before serving. Enjoy this flavorful and perfectly cooked dish!

## Air Fried Chicken Potatoes with Sun-Dried Tomato

**Prep time: 15 minutes | Cook time: 25 minutes | Serves 2**

- 2 teaspoons minced fresh oregano, divided
- 2 teaspoons minced fresh thyme, divided
- 2 teaspoons extra-virgin olive oil, plus extra as needed
- 450 g fingerling potatoes, unpeeled
- 2 (340 g) bone-in split chicken breasts, trimmed
- 1 garlic clove, minced
- 15 g oil-packed sun-dried tomatoes, patted dry and chopped
- 1½ tablespoons red wine vinegar
- 1 tablespoon capers, rinsed and minced
- 1 small shallot, minced
- Salt and ground black pepper, to taste

1. In a large bowl, mix 1 teaspoon of oregano, 1 teaspoon of thyme, ¼ teaspoon of salt, ¼ teaspoon of ground black pepper, and 1 teaspoon of olive oil. Add the potatoes and toss to coat thoroughly. In a separate bowl, combine the chicken with the remaining thyme, oregano, and olive oil. Sprinkle with garlic, salt, and pepper, tossing to coat evenly.
2. Preheat Zone 1 and Zone 2 to 180°C. Place the seasoned potatoes into Zone 1, spreading them out in an even layer. Arrange the chicken pieces on top of the potatoes, ensuring even airflow for cooking.
3. Set the air fryer to cook for 25 minutes. After 12 minutes, pause the cooking cycle, open the basket, and flip the chicken and potatoes for even browning. Reinsert the basket and resume cooking. Check that the chicken reaches an internal temperature of at least 76°C and the potatoes are tender and golden by the end of the cooking time.
4. While the chicken and potatoes cook, prepare the sun-dried tomato mix. In a separate large bowl, combine the sun-dried tomatoes, vinegar, capers, and shallot. Sprinkle with salt and ground black pepper, then toss to mix well.
5. When cooking is complete, carefully remove the chicken and potatoes from the air fryer. Allow them to cool for 10 minutes. Serve warm, paired with the flavorful sun-dried tomato mix. Simple and satisfying!

# Greek Chicken Souvlaki

### Prep time: 30 minutes | Cook time: 15 minutes | Serves 3 to 4

Chicken:
- Grated zest and juice of 1 lemon
- 2 tablespoons extra-virgin olive oil
- 1 tablespoon Greek souvlaki seasoning
- 450 g boneless, skinless chicken breast, cut into 2-inch chunks
- Vegetable oil spray

For Serving:
- Warm pita bread or hot cooked rice
- Sliced ripe tomatoes
- Sliced cucumbers
- Thinly sliced red onion
- Kalamata olives
- Tzatziki

1. In a small bowl, whisk together the lemon zest, lemon juice, olive oil, and souvlaki seasoning to create a flavorful marinade. Place the chicken in a gallon-size resealable plastic bag and pour the marinade over it. Seal the bag, massage to evenly coat the chicken, and place it in a large bowl. Let it marinate for at least 30 minutes at room temperature or up to 24 hours in the refrigerator, turning the bag occasionally to distribute the flavors.
2. Preheat Zone 1 and Zone 2 to 180°C. Arrange the marinated chicken in a single layer in both zones, ensuring there is enough space for proper airflow. Press the MATCH button to ensure both zones operate under the same temperature and timing, then press START/PAUSE to begin cooking.
3. Air fry the chicken at 180°C for 10 minutes. Pause the air fryer halfway through, flip the chicken pieces, and lightly spray them with vegetable oil spray to enhance browning.
4. After the initial cooking, increase the temperature in both zones to 200°C. Cook for an additional 5 minutes to crisp and lightly brown the chicken, ensuring it reaches an internal temperature of at least 76°C.
5. Once cooked, carefully remove the chicken from both zones and transfer it to a serving platter. Pair it with warm pita bread or rice, fresh tomatoes, cucumbers, onions, olives, and tzatziki for a complete and flavorful meal. Enjoy!

# Chicken with Pineapple and Peach

### Prep time: 10 minutes | Cook time: 14 to 15 minutes | Serves 4

- 1 (450 g) low-sodium boneless, skinless chicken breasts, cut into 1-inch pieces
- 1 medium red onion, chopped
- 1 (230 g) tin pineapple chunks, drained, 60 ml juice reserved
- 1 tablespoon peanut oil or safflower oil
- 1 peach, peeled, pitted, and cubed
- 1 tablespoon cornflour
- ½ teaspoon ground ginger
- ¼ teaspoon ground allspice
- Brown rice, cooked (optional)

1. Preheat Zone 1 and Zone 2 to 196°C.
2. In a medium metal bowl that fits the air fryer, mix the chicken, red onion, pineapple, and peanut oil. Divide the mixture evenly between Zone 1 and Zone 2 for balanced cooking.
3. Press the MATCH button to synchronize both zones and bake the chicken mixture for 9 minutes. Open the baskets, stir the contents to ensure even cooking, and return them to the air fryer.
4. Add the peach slices to the chicken mixture in both zones, stir gently, and bake for 3 additional minutes. Open the baskets again and stir to combine the ingredients thoroughly.
5. In a small bowl, whisk together the reserved pineapple juice, cornflour, ginger, and allspice until smooth. Pour the mixture over the chicken in both zones and stir to coat evenly.
6. Return the baskets to the air fryer and bake for another 2 to 3 minutes, or until the chicken reaches an internal temperature of 76°C and the sauce thickens slightly.
7. Remove the chicken mixture from both zones and serve immediately over hot cooked brown rice, if desired. Enjoy the flavorful combination of sweet and savory!

# Korean Flavour Glazed Chicken Wings

**Prep time: 10 minutes | Cook time: 25 minutes | Serves 4**

Wings:
- 900 g chicken wings
- 1 teaspoon salt
- 1 teaspoon ground black pepper

Sauce:
- 2 tablespoons gochujang
- 1 tablespoon mayonnaise
- 1 tablespoon minced ginger
- 1 tablespoon minced garlic
- 1 teaspoon agave nectar
- 2 packets Splenda
- 1 tablespoon sesame oil

For Garnish:
- 2 teaspoons sesame seeds
- 15 g chopped green onions

1. Preheat Zone 1 and Zone 2 to 200°C. Line two baking pans with aluminum foil, placing a rack on each pan for even airflow.
2. On a clean work surface, season the chicken wings with salt and ground black pepper. Arrange half of the wings on the rack in Zone 1 and the other half on the rack in Zone 2, ensuring the wings are spread out for even cooking.
3. Set the temperature in both zones to 200°C and cook for 20 minutes. Use the SMART FINISH button to ensure both zones finish simultaneously. Flip the wings halfway through to promote even browning.
4. While the wings cook, prepare the sauce by combining the ingredients in a small bowl. Stir until smooth, then divide the sauce into two portions, reserving half for serving.
5. Once the wings are golden brown, remove them from the air fryer and toss with the remaining half of the sauce to coat thoroughly.
6. Return the sauced wings to Zone 1 and Zone 2. Cook at 200°C for an additional 5 minutes, or until the wings are caramelized and their internal temperature reaches at least 76°C.
7. Transfer the wings to a large plate and sprinkle with sesame seeds and chopped green onions. Serve with the reserved sauce for dipping. Enjoy these perfectly glazed, flavorful wings!

# Chapter 6
## Beef, Pork, and Lamb

# Chapter 5 Beef, Pork, and Lamb

## Banger and Peppers

**Prep time: 7 minutes | Cook time: 35 minutes | Serves 4**

- Oil, for spraying
- 900 g hot or sweet Italian-seasoned banger links, cut into thick slices
- 4 large peppers of any color, seeded and cut into slices
- 1 onion, thinly sliced
- 1 tablespoon olive oil
- 1 tablespoon chopped fresh parsley
- 1 teaspoon dried oregano
- 1 teaspoon dried basil
- 1 teaspoon balsamic vinegar

1. Line Zone 1 and Zone 2 with parchment paper and spray lightly with oil.
2. In a large bowl, mix the banger, peppers, and onion.
3. In a small bowl, whisk olive oil, parsley, oregano, basil, and balsamic vinegar. Pour over the banger mixture and toss until evenly coated.
4. Use a slotted spoon to transfer the mixture to Zone 1 and Zone 2, ensuring excess liquid is drained. Arrange in a single layer.
5. Select AIR FRY, set the temperature to 180°C, and cook for 20 minutes. Stir the mixture, then cook for an additional 15 minutes, or until the banger is browned and the juices run clear.
6. Serve warm and enjoy the flavorful, roasted banger and vegetables.

## Spicy Tomato Beef Meatballs

**Prep time: 10 minutes | Cook time: 15 minutes | Serves 4**

- 3 spring onions, minced
- 1 garlic clove, minced
- 1 egg yolk
- 60 ml cream cracker crumbs
- Pinch salt
- Freshly ground black pepper, to taste
- 450 g 95% lean beef mince
- Olive oil spray
- 300 ml any tomato pasta sauce
- 2 tablespoons Dijon mustard

1. In a large bowl, mix the spring onion, garlic, egg yolk, cracker crumbs, salt, and pepper until well combined.
2. Add the beef and gently mix by hand until fully combined. Shape the mixture into 1½-inch round meatballs.
3. Preheat Zone 1 and Zone 2 by selecting BAKE, setting the temperature to 200°C, and the time to 3 minutes. Press START/PAUSE to begin.
4. Once preheated, spray the crisper plates in Zone 1 and Zone 2 with olive oil. Divide the meatballs evenly between the zones, ensuring they are placed in a single layer without touching. Spray the meatballs lightly with olive oil.
5. Select BAKE, set the temperature to 200°C, and cook for 11 minutes. Press MATCH to synchronize both zones and press START/PAUSE.
6. Check that the meatballs are cooked to 74°C using a food thermometer. Transfer the cooked meatballs to a 6-inch metal bowl.
7. Repeat the cooking process with any remaining meatballs.
8. Top the cooked meatballs with pasta sauce and Dijon mustard, then mix gently. Place the bowl into Zone 1.
9. Select BAKE, set the temperature to 200°C, and cook for 4 minutes. Press START/PAUSE to begin.
10. Once done, serve the meatballs hot and enjoy!

## Green Pepper Cheeseburgers

**Prep time: 5 minutes | Cook time: 30 minutes | Serves 4**

- 2 green peppers
- 680 g 85% lean beef mince
- 1 clove garlic, minced
- 1 teaspoon salt
- ½ teaspoon freshly ground black pepper
- 4 slices Cheddar cheese (about 85 g)
- 4 large lettuce leaves

1. Preheat Zone 1 to 200°C. Arrange the peppers in Zone 1 and select AIR FRY. Cook for 20 minutes, turning halfway through, until softened and slightly charred. Transfer the peppers to a bowl, cover with a plate, and let cool. Peel off the skin, remove seeds and stems, slice into strips, and set aside.
2. In a large bowl, mix the beef with garlic, salt, and pepper. Shape into 4 patties.
3. Lower Zone 1 to 180°C. Arrange the patties in a single layer and select AIR FRY. Cook for 10 minutes, flipping halfway through, until the internal temperature reaches 72°C.
4. Add cheese slices to the patties and air fry for 1 to 2 minutes more until the cheese melts.
5. Serve the burgers on lettuce leaves topped with roasted peppers. Enjoy!

## Beef Burger

**Prep time: 20 minutes | Cook time: 12 minutes | Serves 4**

- 570 g lean beef mince
- 1 tablespoon soy sauce or tamari
- 1 teaspoon Dijon mustard
- ½ teaspoon smoked paprika
- 1 teaspoon shallot powder
- 1 clove garlic, minced
- ½ teaspoon cumin powder
- 60 g spring onions, minced
- ⅓ teaspoon sea salt flakes
- ⅓ teaspoon freshly cracked mixed peppercorns
- 1 teaspoon celery salt
- 1 teaspoon dried parsley

1. Combine all the ingredients in a bowl and knead until fully mixed.
2. Shape the mixture into four patties, pressing a shallow dip into the center of each to prevent puffing during cooking.
3. Spritz the patties with nonstick cooking spray on all sides.
4. Arrange the patties in Zone 1 and Zone 2 of the air fryer. Select AIR FRY, set the temperature to 180°C, and cook for 12 minutes.
5. Check for doneness with an instant-read thermometer; the patties should reach 72°C. Serve warm. Bon appétit!

## Beef Mince Taco Rolls

**Prep time: 20 minutes | Cook time: 10 minutes | Serves 4**

- 230 g 80/20 beef mince
- 80 ml water
- 1 tablespoon chilli powder
- 2 teaspoons cumin
- ½ teaspoon garlic powder
- ¼ teaspoon dried oregano
- 60 g tinned diced tomatoes
- 2 tablespoons chopped coriander
- 355 g shredded Mozzarella cheese
- 60 g blanched finely ground almond flour
- 60 g full-fat cream cheese
- 1 large egg

1. In a frying pan over medium heat, cook the beef mince for 7 to 10 minutes until browned. Drain off any excess fat.
2. Stir in water, chili powder, cumin, garlic powder, oregano, tomatoes, and coriander. Bring the mixture to a boil, then reduce the heat and simmer for 3 minutes.
3. In a large microwave-safe bowl, combine Mozzarella, almond flour, cream cheese, and egg. Microwave for 1 minute, then stir until the mixture forms a smooth dough.
4. On a piece of parchment paper, press the dough into a large rectangle. Wet your hands as needed to prevent sticking. Cut the dough into eight rectangles.
5. Spoon a few tablespoons of the meat mixture onto each rectangle. Fold the short ends toward the center, then roll lengthwise like a burrito to seal the filling.
6. Line Zone 1 and Zone 2 of the air fryer with parchment paper. Place the taco rolls in a single layer in each zone.
7. Select AIR FRY, set the temperature to 180°C, and cook for 10 minutes, flipping halfway through.
8. Let the taco rolls cool for 10 minutes before serving. Enjoy the crispy and flavorful rolls!

## Beef Bavette Steak with Sage

**Prep time: 13 minutes | Cook time: 7 minutes | Serves 2**

- 80 ml sour cream
- 120 g spring onion, chopped
- 1 tablespoon mayonnaise
- 3 cloves garlic, smashed
- 450 g beef bavette or skirt steak, trimmed and cubed
- 2 tablespoons fresh sage, minced
- ½ teaspoon salt
- ⅓ teaspoon black pepper, or to taste

1. Season the beef cubes with salt and pepper, then arrange them in a baking dish that fits in Zone 1.
2. Add spring onions and garlic to the beef. Select AIR FRY, set the temperature to 200°C, and cook for 7 minutes.
3. Once the beef begins to tender, stir in the cream, mayonnaise, and sage. Return to Zone 1 and air fry for an additional 8 minutes.
4. Serve hot and enjoy. Bon appétit!

## Mustard Herb Pork Tenderloin

**Prep time: 5 minutes | Cook time: 20 minutes | Serves 6**

- 60 ml mayonnaise
- 2 tablespoons Dijon mustard
- ½ teaspoon dried thyme
- ¼ teaspoon dried rosemary
- 1 (450 g) pork tenderloin
- ½ teaspoon salt
- ¼ teaspoon ground black pepper

1. In a small bowl, mix mayonnaise, mustard, thyme, and rosemary. Brush the mixture evenly over all sides of the tenderloin, then sprinkle with salt and pepper.
2. Place the tenderloin in Zone 1 or Zone 2 of the air fryer. Select AIR FRY, set the temperature to 200°C, and cook for 20 minutes, turning halfway through.
3. Check that the tenderloin is golden and reaches an internal temperature of at least 64°C. Serve warm and enjoy!

## Sumptuous Pizza Tortilla Rolls

**Prep time: 10 minutes | Cook time: 6 minutes | Serves 4**

- 1 teaspoon butter
- ½ medium onion, slivered
- ½ red or green pepper, julienned
- 110 g fresh white mushrooms, chopped
- 120 ml pizza sauce
- 8 flour tortillas
- 8 thin slices wafer-thin ham
- 24 pepperoni slices
- 235 g shredded Mozzarella cheese
- Cooking spray

1. Preheat Zone 1 to 200ºC.
2. Place butter, onions, peppers, and mushrooms in a baking tray. Bake in Zone 1 for 3 minutes, then stir and cook for another 3 to 4 minutes until crisp and tender. Remove and set aside.
3. Spread 2 teaspoons of pizza sauce on one half of each tortilla. Add a slice of ham, 3 slices of pepperoni, sautéed vegetables, and cheese.
4. Roll up the tortillas tightly, secure with toothpicks if needed, and spray with oil.
5. Place 4 rolls in Zone 1 and select AIR FRY. Cook at 200ºC for 4 minutes, then turn and cook for another 4 minutes until heated through and lightly browned.
6. Repeat the process for the remaining rolls.
7. Serve immediately and enjoy the crispy, cheesy pizza rolls!

## Spaghetti Zoodles and Meatballs

**Prep time: 30 minutes | Cook time: 11 to 13 minutes | Serves 6**

- 450 g beef mince
- 1½ teaspoons sea salt, plus more for seasoning
- 1 large egg, beaten
- 1 teaspoon gelatin
- 180 g Parmesan cheese
- 2 teaspoons minced garlic
- 1 teaspoon Italian seasoning
- Freshly ground black pepper, to taste
- Avocado oil spray
- Keto-friendly marinara sauce, for serving
- 170 g courgette noodles, made using a spiralizer or store-bought

1. Place the beef mince in a large bowl and season with salt.
2. In a separate bowl, sprinkle gelatin over the egg and let sit for 5 minutes.
3. Stir the gelatin mixture, pour it over the beef, and add Parmesan, garlic, and Italian seasoning. Season with salt and pepper, then mix thoroughly.
4. Form the mixture into 1½-inch meatballs, place them on a plate, cover with cling film, and refrigerate for at least 1 hour or overnight.
5. Spray the meatballs with oil. Arrange them in Zone 1 of the air fryer in a single layer. Select AIR FRY, set to 200ºC, and cook for 4 minutes. Flip the meatballs, spray with more oil, and air fry for another 4 minutes, or until an instant-read thermometer registers 72ºC. Transfer to a plate to rest.
6. While the meatballs rest, heat marinara sauce in a saucepan over medium heat.
7. Place courgette noodles in Zone 2 of the air fryer. Select AIR FRY, set to 200ºC, and cook for 3 to 5 minutes until tender.
8. To serve, place the courgette noodles in bowls, top with meatballs, and spoon warm marinara over them. Enjoy!

## Five-Spice Pork Belly

**Prep time: 10 minutes | Cook time: 17 minutes | Serves 4**

- 450 g unsalted pork belly

Sauce:
- 1 tablespoon coconut oil
- 1 (1-inch) piece fresh ginger, peeled and grated
- 2 cloves garlic, minced
- 120 ml beef or chicken stock
- 2 teaspoons Chinese five-spice powder
- ¼ to 120 ml liquid or powdered sweetener
- 3 tablespoons wheat-free tamari
- 1 spring onion, sliced, plus more for garnish

1. Spray Zone 1 and Zone 2 with avocado oil and preheat to 200ºC.
2. Slice the pork belly into ½-inch-thick pieces and season all sides with five-spice powder. Arrange the slices in a single layer in Zone 1 and Zone 2. Select AIR FRY, set to 200ºC, and cook for 8 minutes, flipping halfway through, until golden and cooked to your liking.
3. While the pork belly cooks, heat coconut oil in a small saucepan over medium heat. Sauté ginger and garlic for 1 minute until fragrant. Add stock, sweetener, and tamari, then simmer for 10 to 15 minutes until thickened. Stir in spring onions and cook for 1 minute until softened. Adjust seasoning as needed.
4. Transfer the cooked pork belly to a large bowl, pour the sauce over it, and toss to coat evenly. Arrange the slices on a serving platter and garnish with additional spring onions.
5. Serve immediately for best flavor. Store leftovers in an airtight container in the fridge for up to 4 days. Reheat in the air fryer at 200ºC for 3 minutes, or until heated through.

# Italian Bangers with Peppers and Onions

**Prep time: 5 minutes | Cook time: 28 minutes | Serves 3**

- 1 medium onion, thinly sliced
- 1 yellow or orange pepper, thinly sliced
- 1 red pepper, thinly sliced
- 60 ml avocado oil or melted coconut oil
- 1 teaspoon fine sea salt
- 6 Italian-seasoned bangers
- Dijon mustard, for serving (optional)

1. Preheat Zone 1 and Zone 2 to 200°C.
2. In a large bowl, toss the onion and peppers with oil until evenly coated. Season with salt. Divide the veggies evenly between Zone 1 and Zone 2, placing them in pie dishes.
3. Select AIR FRY for both zones, set the temperature to 200°C, and cook the veggies for 8 minutes, stirring halfway through. Remove the pie dishes and set the veggies aside.
4. Spray the baskets of Zone 1 and Zone 2 with avocado oil. Divide the bangers evenly between the two zones and arrange in a single layer.
5. Select AIR FRY, set the temperature to 200°C, and cook for 20 minutes, flipping the bangers halfway through.
6. In the final 2 minutes of cooking, return the pie dishes with the onion and peppers to Zone 1 and Zone 2 to reheat.
7. Transfer the veggies to a serving platter and arrange the crispy bangers on top. Serve with Dijon mustard, if desired.
8. Store leftovers in an airtight container in the fridge for up to 7 days or in the freezer for up to a month. Reheat in a preheated 200°C air fryer for 3 minutes, or until warmed through. Enjoy!

# Lamb Chops with Horseradish Sauce

**Prep time: 30 minutes | Cook time: 13 minutes | Serves 4**

Lamb:
- 4 lamb loin chops
- 2 tablespoons vegetable oil
- 1 clove garlic, minced

Horseradish Cream Sauce:
- 120 ml mayonnaise
- 1 tablespoon Dijon mustard
- 1 to 1½ tablespoons grated horseradish
- 2 teaspoons sugar
- Vegetable oil spray
- ½ teaspoon coarse or flaky salt
- ½ teaspoon black pepper

1. Brush the lamb chops with oil, rub with garlic, and season evenly with salt and pepper. Let them marinate at room temperature for 30 minutes.
2. While the lamb marinates, prepare the sauce: In a medium bowl, mix mayonnaise, mustard, horseradish, and sugar until smooth. Reserve half of the sauce for serving.
3. Preheat Zone 1 to 160°C and spray the basket with vegetable oil spray. Place the lamb chops in a single layer in Zone 1. Select AIR FRY and cook for 10 minutes, flipping the chops halfway through.
4. Remove the chops and toss them in the bowl with the horseradish sauce, coating evenly. Return the chops to Zone 1, increase the temperature to 200°C, and air fry for 3 minutes. Use a meat thermometer to check that the internal temperature reaches 64°C for medium-rare.
5. Serve the chops hot with the reserved horseradish sauce on the side. Enjoy the tender and flavorful lamb!

# Pork Kebab with Yoghurt Sauce

**Prep time: 25 minutes | Cook time: 12 minutes | Serves 4**

- 2 teaspoons olive oil
- 230 g pork mince
- 230 g beef mince
- 1 egg, whisked
- Sea salt and ground black pepper, to taste

Yoghurt Sauce:
- 2 tablespoons olive oil
- 2 tablespoons fresh lemon juice
- Sea salt, to taste
- 1 teaspoon paprika
- 2 garlic cloves, minced
- 1 teaspoon dried marjoram
- 1 teaspoon mustard seeds
- ½ teaspoon celery salt
- ¼ teaspoon red pepper flakes, crushed
- 120 ml full-fat yoghurt
- 1 teaspoon dried dill

1. Spritz the sides and bottom of Zone 1 with 2 teaspoons of olive oil to prevent sticking.
2. In a mixing bowl, combine the pork, beef, egg, salt, black pepper, paprika, garlic, marjoram, mustard seeds, and celery salt. Mix thoroughly until evenly combined.
3. Shape the mixture into kebabs and place them in Zone 1 in a single layer. Select AIR FRY, set the temperature to 190°C, and cook for 11 to 12 minutes, turning the kebabs once or twice for even browning. Press START/PAUSE to begin.
4. While the kebabs cook, mix all the sauce ingredients in a small bowl. Refrigerate until ready to serve.
5. Once the kebabs are fully cooked, transfer them to a serving platter. Serve hot with the chilled yogurt sauce on the side. Enjoy the flavorful and tender kebabs!

## Cheese Pork Chops

**Prep time: 15 minutes | Cook time: 9 to 14 minutes | Serves 4**

- 2 large eggs
- 120 g finely grated Parmesan cheese
- 60 g finely ground blanched almond flour or finely crushed pork scratchings
- 1 teaspoon paprika
- ½ teaspoon dried oregano
- ½ teaspoon garlic powder
- Salt and freshly ground black pepper, to taste
- 570 g (1-inch-thick) boneless pork chops
- Avocado oil spray

1. Beat the eggs in a shallow bowl. In another bowl, mix Parmesan, almond flour, paprika, oregano, garlic powder, salt, and pepper.
2. Dip the pork chops in the eggs, coat with the Parmesan mixture, and spray lightly with oil.
3. Preheat Zone 1 and Zone 2 by selecting BAKE, setting the temperature to 200ºC, and pressing START/PAUSE.
4. Place the pork chops in a single layer in both zones. Spray the tops with oil.
5. Select BAKE, set to 200ºC, and cook for 6 minutes. Flip, spray again, and cook for another 3 to 8 minutes until a thermometer reads 64ºC.
6. Let the pork chops rest for 5 minutes before serving. Enjoy!

## Reuben Beef Rolls with Thousand Island Sauce

**Prep time: 15 minutes | Cook time: 10 minutes per batch | Makes 10 rolls**

- 230 g cooked salt beef, chopped
- 120 g drained and chopped sauerkraut
- 1 (230 g) package cream cheese, softened
- 120 g shredded Swiss cheese
- 20 slices prosciutto
- Cooking spray
- Thousand Island Sauce:
- 60 g chopped dill pickles
- 60 ml tomato ketchup
- 180 ml mayonnaise
- Fresh thyme leaves, for garnish
- 2 tablespoons sugar
- ⅛ teaspoon fine sea salt
- Ground black pepper, to taste

1. Preheat Zone 1 and Zone 2 to 200ºC and spritz with cooking spray.
2. In a large bowl, combine beef, sauerkraut, cream cheese, and Swiss cheese. Stir until well mixed.
3. Unroll one slice of prosciutto on a clean surface and place another slice crosswise. Scoop 4 tablespoons of the beef mixture and place it in the center.
4. Fold the sides of the top prosciutto slice over the filling, then roll the long sides of the bottom prosciutto around the mixture to form a roll, overlapping the edges by about 1 inch. Repeat with the remaining filling and prosciutto.
5. Arrange the rolls in Zone 1 and Zone 2, seam side down. Spritz with cooking spray.
6. Select AIR FRY, set to 200ºC, and cook for 10 minutes, flipping halfway through. Work in batches to avoid overcrowding.
7. While the rolls cook, mix the dipping sauce ingredients in a small bowl and stir to combine.
8. Serve the prosciutto rolls with the dipping sauce on the side. Enjoy!

## Cantonese BBQ Pork

**Prep time: 30 minutes | Cook time: 15 minutes | Serves 4**

- 60 ml honey
- 2 tablespoons dark soy sauce
- 1 tablespoon sugar
- 1 tablespoon Shaoxing wine (rice cooking wine)
- 1 tablespoon hoisin sauce
- 2 teaspoons minced garlic
- 2 teaspoons minced fresh ginger
- 1 teaspoon Chinese five-spice powder
- 450 g fatty pork shoulder, cut into long, 1-inch-thick pieces

1. In a small microwave-safe bowl, mix honey, soy sauce, sugar, wine, hoisin, garlic, ginger, and five-spice powder. Microwave in 10-second intervals, stirring in between, until the honey dissolves.
2. Pierce the pork slices with a fork to help the marinade penetrate. Place the pork in a large bowl or resealable bag and pour in half the marinade. Reserve the other half for the sauce. Toss the pork to coat, then marinate at room temperature for 30 minutes or refrigerate for up to 24 hours.
3. Arrange the pork in a single layer in Zone 1 and Zone 2. Select AIR FRY, set the temperature to 200ºC, and cook for 15 minutes. Flip and baste the pork halfway through with some of the reserved marinade.
4. While the pork cooks, microwave the remaining marinade on high for 45 to 60 seconds, stirring every 15 seconds, until it thickens slightly into a sauce.
5. Transfer the cooked pork to a cutting board and let it rest for 10 minutes. Brush with the thickened sauce and serve.

## Steak Gyro Platter

**Prep time: 30 minutes | Cook time: 8 to 10 minutes | Serves 4**

- 450 g bavette or skirt steak
- 1 teaspoon garlic powder
- 1 teaspoon ground cumin
- ½ teaspoon sea salt
- ½ teaspoon freshly ground black pepper
- 140 g shredded romaine lettuce
- 120 g crumbled feta cheese
- 120 g peeled and diced cucumber
- 80 g sliced red onion
- 60 g seeded and diced tomato
- 2 tablespoons pitted and sliced black olives
- Tzatziki sauce, for serving

1. Pat the steak dry with paper towels. Mix garlic powder, cumin, salt, and pepper in a small bowl. Sprinkle evenly over the steak and let it rest at room temperature for 45 minutes.
2. Preheat Zone 1 to 200°C. Place the steak in Zone 1 and select AIR FRY. Cook for 4 minutes, then flip and cook for an additional 4 to 6 minutes, until the thickest point reads 49°C for medium-rare (or to your preferred doneness). Remove the steak and let it rest for 5 minutes.
3. Arrange the romaine on plates and top with feta, cucumber, red onion, tomato, and olives. Slice the steak and serve alongside the salad. Enjoy!

## Onion Pork Kebabs

**Prep time: 22 minutes | Cook time: 18 minutes | Serves 3**

- 2 tablespoons tomato purée
- ½ fresh green chilli, minced
- ⅓ teaspoon paprika
- 450 g pork mince
- 120 g spring onions, finely chopped
- 3 cloves garlic, peeled and finely minced
- 1 teaspoon ground black pepper, or more to taste
- 1 teaspoon salt, or more to taste

1. Thoroughly combine all ingredients in a mixing bowl, then shape the mixture into banger shapes.
2. Preheat Zone 1 and Zone 2 to 180°C and arrange the kebabs in a single layer in both zones. Select AIR FRY, set the temperature to 180°C, and cook for 18 minutes, flipping halfway through.
3. While the kebabs cook, mound the salad on a serving platter.
4. Once the kebabs are done, place them on top of the salad and serve warm. Bon appétit!

## Macadamia Nuts Crusted Pork Rack & Italian Lamb Chops with Avocado Mayo

**Prep time: 5 minutes | Cook time: 35 minutes | Serves 2**

### Macadamia Nuts Crusted Pork Rack | Serves 2

- 1 clove garlic, minced
- 2 tablespoons olive oil
- 450 g rack of pork
- 235 g chopped macadamia nuts
- 1 tablespoon breadcrumbs
- 1 tablespoon rosemary, chopped
- 1 egg
- Salt and ground black pepper, to taste

### Italian Lamb Chops with Avocado Mayo | Serves 2

- 2 lamp chops
- 2 teaspoons Italian herbs
- 2 avocados
- 120 ml mayonnaise
- 1 tablespoon lemon juice

**For Macadamia Nuts Crusted Pork Rack:**

1. Preheat Zone 1 to 180°C.
2. Mix the garlic and olive oil in a small bowl.
3. On a clean surface, rub the pork rack with the garlic oil and season both sides with salt and black pepper.
4. Combine macadamia nuts, breadcrumbs, and rosemary in a shallow dish. Whisk the egg in a separate bowl.
5. Dip the pork in the egg, then coat it with the macadamia nut mixture, pressing gently to adhere. Shake off any excess.
6. Place the pork in Zone 1. Select AIR FRY, set to 180°C, and cook for 30 minutes, flipping halfway through. Increase the temperature to 200°C and cook for an additional 5 minutes, or until the pork is browned and fully cooked.
7. Serve immediately and enjoy!

**For Italian Lamb Chops with Avocado Mayo:**

1. Season the lamb chops with Italian herbs and let rest for 5 minutes.
2. Preheat Zone 2 to 200°C and place the rack inside.
3. Arrange the lamb chops on the rack and select AIR FRY. Cook for 12 minutes, flipping halfway through for even browning.
4. While the chops cook, halve the avocados, remove the pits, and scoop the flesh into a blender.
5. Add mayonnaise and lemon juice, then blend until smooth and creamy.
6. Carefully remove the chops from Zone 2, plate them, and serve with the avocado mayo. Enjoy!

## Greek-Style Meatloaf

**Prep time: 5 minutes | Cook time: 25 minutes | Serves 6**

- 450 g lean beef mince
- 2 eggs
- 2 plum tomatoes, diced
- ½ brown onion, diced
- 60 g whole wheat bread crumbs
- 1 teaspoon garlic powder
- 1 teaspoon dried oregano
- 1 teaspoon dried thyme
- 1 teaspoon salt
- 1 teaspoon black pepper
- 60 g mozzarella cheese, shredded
- 1 tablespoon olive oil
- Fresh chopped parsley, for garnish

1. Preheat Zone 1 and Zone 2 to 190ºC.
2. In a large bowl, combine the beef, eggs, tomatoes, onion, bread crumbs, garlic powder, oregano, thyme, salt, pepper, and cheese. Stir to mix well.
3. Shape the mixture into a loaf, then flatten it to about 1 inch thick.
4. Brush the top with olive oil and place the meatloaf in the preheated air fryer basket in Zone 1 or Zone 2. Select AIR FRY, set to 190ºC, and cook for 25 minutes. Press START/PAUSE to begin.
5. Once done, remove the meatloaf from the air fryer and let it rest for 5 minutes before slicing. Serve with a sprinkle of parsley.

## Ham with Sweet Potatoes

**Prep time: 20 minutes | Cook time: 15 to 17 minutes | Serves 4**

- 235 g freshly squeezed orange juice
- 96 g packed light brown sugar
- 1 tablespoon Dijon mustard
- ½ teaspoon salt
- ½ teaspoon freshly ground black pepper
- 3 sweet potatoes, cut into small wedges
- 2 gammon steaks (230 g each), halved

1 to 2 tablespoons oil

1. In a large bowl, whisk together orange juice, brown sugar, Dijon, salt, and pepper until well blended. Toss the sweet potato wedges in the brown sugar mixture until coated.
2. Preheat Zone 1 and Zone 2 to 200ºC. Line the baskets with parchment paper and spritz with oil. Press START/PAUSE to begin preheating.
3. Place the sweet potato wedges on the parchment in both zones, spreading them out evenly.
4. Select AIR FRY, set to 200ºC, and cook for 10 minutes.
5. Place the gammon steaks on top of the sweet potatoes and brush everything with more of the orange juice mixture.
6. Cook for 3 minutes, then flip the gammon steaks and cook for an additional 2 to 4 minutes, or until the sweet potatoes are soft and the glaze has thickened.
7. Once cooked, cut the gammon steaks in half and serve on top of the sweet potatoes. Enjoy this delicious and flavorful meal!

## Bo Luc Lac

**Prep time: 50 minutes | Cook time: 8 minutes | Serves 4**

Meat:
- 2 teaspoons soy sauce
- 4 garlic cloves, minced
- 1 teaspoon coarse or flaky salt
- 2 teaspoons sugar
- ¼ teaspoon ground black pepper
- 1 teaspoon toasted sesame oil
- 680 g top rump steak, cut into 1-inch cubes
- Cooking spray

Salad:
- 1 head butterhead lettuce, leaves separated and torn into large pieces
- 60 g fresh mint leaves
- 120 g halved baby plum tomatoes
- ½ red onion, halved and thinly sliced
- 2 tablespoons apple cider vinegar
- 1 garlic clove, minced
- 2 teaspoons sugar
- ¼ teaspoon coarse or flaky salt
- ¼ teaspoon ground black pepper
- 2 tablespoons vegetable oil

Serving:
- Lime wedges, for garnish
- Coarse salt and freshly cracked black pepper, to taste

1. In a large bowl, combine all the ingredients for the meat except for the steak. Stir well to mix.
2. Dunk the steak cubes into the mixture, pressing to coat evenly. Cover the bowl with plastic wrap and marinate at room temperature for at least 30 minutes.
3. Preheat Zone 1 and Zone 2 to 230ºC. Spritz the baskets with cooking spray.
4. Discard the marinade and divide the steak cubes evenly between Zone 1 and Zone 2, arranging them in a single layer to avoid overcrowding.
5. Select AIR FRY, set the temperature to 230ºC, and cook for 4 minutes. Shake both baskets halfway through cooking. The steak cubes should be lightly browned but still a little pink inside. Press START/PAUSE to begin.
6. While the steak cooks, combine all the salad ingredients in a large bowl and toss to mix well.
7. Transfer the salad to a large serving bowl and top with the cooked steak cubes. Squeeze lime wedges over the top and sprinkle with salt and black pepper before serving. Enjoy!

## Short Ribs with Chimichurri

**Prep time: 30 minutes | Cook time: 13 minutes | Serves 4**

- 450 g boneless short ribs
- 1½ teaspoons sea salt, divided
- ½ teaspoon freshly ground black pepper, divided
- 120 g fresh parsley leaves
- 120 g fresh coriander leaves
- 1 teaspoon minced garlic
- 1 tablespoon freshly squeezed lemon juice
- ½ teaspoon ground cumin
- ¼ teaspoon red pepper flakes
- 2 tablespoons extra-virgin olive oil
- Avocado oil spray

1. Pat the short ribs dry with paper towels. Season all sides with 1 teaspoon salt and ¼ teaspoon black pepper. Let sit at room temperature for 45 minutes.
2. While the ribs rest, combine parsley, coriander, garlic, lemon juice, cumin, red pepper flakes, the remaining ½ teaspoon salt, and ¼ teaspoon black pepper in a blender or food processor. With the blender running, slowly drizzle in the olive oil. Blend for 1 minute until smooth and well combined.
3. Preheat Zone 1 to 200°C. Spray both sides of the ribs with oil and place them in the basket. Select AIR FRY and cook for 8 minutes. Flip the ribs and cook for an additional 5 minutes, or until an instant-read thermometer reads 52°C for medium-rare (or to your desired doneness).
4. Let the meat rest for 5 to 10 minutes before slicing. Serve with chimichurri sauce and enjoy!

## Beefy Poppers

**Prep time: 15 minutes | Cook time: 15 minutes | Makes 8 poppers**

- 8 medium red chillis, stemmed, halved, and seeded
- 1 (230 g) package cream cheese (or cream cheese style spread for dairy-free), softened
- 900 g beef mince (85% lean)
- 1 teaspoon fine sea salt
- ½ teaspoon ground black pepper
- 8 slices thin-cut bacon
- Fresh coriander leaves, for garnish

1. Spray both baskets of the Ninja Double Stack Air Fryer with avocado oil to ensure non-stick cooking surfaces. Preheat the appliance to 200°C using the MATCH button, pressing START/PAUSE to activate the synchronized preheating process.
2. Stuff each jalapeño half with a few tablespoons of cream cheese, then press the halves back together to recreate a whole jalapeño. Prepare all 8 jalapeños in this manner.
3. Season the beef mince with salt and pepper, mixing thoroughly with your hands until well incorporated. Take about 110 g of the seasoned beef, flatten it in your palm, and position a stuffed jalapeño at the center. Wrap the beef around the jalapeño to form an egg shape, ensuring it's fully enclosed. Wrap a rasher of bacon around each beef-covered jalapeño and secure it in place with a toothpick.
4. Divide the prepared jalapeños evenly between Zone 1 and Zone 2 of the Ninja Double Stack Air Fryer, leaving enough space around each for proper air circulation. Select the MATCH button to synchronize both zones, set the temperature to 200°C, and air fry for 15 minutes or until the bacon is crispy and the beef is cooked through.
5. Carefully remove the jalapeños from both baskets and garnish them with freshly chopped coriander before serving.
6. Store any leftovers in an airtight container in the fridge for up to 3 days or in the freezer for a maximum of 1 month. When reheating, preheat the air fryer to 180°C, place the jalapeños in one of the baskets, and heat for 4 minutes or until thoroughly warmed and the bacon is crisp.

## Honey-Baked Pork Loin

**Prep time: 30 minutes | Cook time: 22 to 25 minutes | Serves 6**

- 60 ml honey
- 60 g freshly squeezed lemon juice
- 2 tablespoons soy sauce
- 1 teaspoon garlic powder
- 1 (900 g) pork loin
- 2 tablespoons vegetable oil

1. In a medium bowl, whisk together honey, lemon juice, soy sauce, and garlic powder. Reserve half the mixture for basting.
2. Cut 5 slits into the pork loin, place it in a resealable bag, and add the remaining marinade. Seal and refrigerate for at least 2 hours.
3. Preheat Zone 1 to 200°C and line the basket with parchment paper.
4. Remove the pork from the marinade and place it on the parchment. Spritz with oil and baste with some of the reserved marinade.
5. Select AIR FRY and cook for 15 minutes. Flip the pork, baste with more marinade, spritz with oil again, and cook for an additional 7 to 10 minutes, or until the internal temperature reaches 64°C.
6. Let the pork rest for 5 minutes before slicing and serving. Enjoy the flavorful, juicy pork!

## Southern Chilli

**Prep time: 20 minutes | Cook time: 25 minutes | Serves 4**

- 450 g beef mince (85% lean)
- 235 g minced onion
- 1 (794 g) tin tomato purée
- 1 (425 g) tin diced tomatoes
- 1 (425 g) tin red kidney beans, rinsed and drained
- 60 g Chili seasoning

1. Preheat Zone 1 and Zone 2 to 200°C.
2. Divide the beef mince and minced onion evenly between two baking trays. Place one tray in Zone 1 and the other in Zone 2. Select AIR FRY and cook for 4 minutes. Open both zones, stir the mixtures, and cook for another 4 minutes until browned. Remove the trays, drain the meat, and transfer the contents to a large bowl.
3. Reduce the temperature of both zones to 180°C.
4. To the bowl with the cooked meat, add the tomato purée, diced tomatoes, kidney beans, and chili seasoning. Mix well, then divide the mixture evenly between the two trays.
5. Place the trays back in Zone 1 and Zone 2. Select AIR FRY, set to 180°C, and cook for 25 minutes, stirring each tray every 10 minutes, until the chili thickens to your desired consistency.
6. Once done, remove the trays from the air fryer and serve the chili warm. Enjoy a hearty and flavorful dish!

## Blackened Cajun Pork Roast

**Prep time: 20 minutes | Cook time: 33 minutes | Serves 4**

- 900 g bone-in pork loin roast
- 2 tablespoons oil
- 60 ml Cajun seasoning
- 120 g diced onion
- 120 g diced celery
- 120 g diced green pepper
- 1 tablespoon minced garlic

1. Cut 5 slits across the pork roast and spritz it with oil to coat completely. Sprinkle evenly with Cajun seasoning.
2. In a bowl, mix onion, celery, green pepper, and garlic until combined. Set aside.
3. Preheat Zone 1 to 180°C and line it with parchment paper.
4. Place the pork roast on the parchment and spritz with oil. Select AIR FRY, set to 180°C, and press START/PAUSE. Cook for 5 minutes, flip, and repeat in 5-minute increments for a total of 20 minutes.
5. Increase the temperature to 200°C. Cook the roast for 8 minutes, flip, then add the vegetable mixture to Zone 1. Cook for an additional 5 minutes.
6. Let the pork roast rest for 5 minutes before slicing. Serve with the roasted vegetables. Enjoy!

## Smoky Pork Tenderloin

**Prep time: 5 minutes | Cook time: 19 to 22 minutes | Serves 6**

- 680 g pork tenderloin
- 1 tablespoon avocado oil
- 1 teaspoon chilli powder
- 1 teaspoon smoked paprika
- 1 teaspoon garlic powder
- 1 teaspoon sea salt
- 1 teaspoon freshly ground black pepper

1. Use a fork to pierce the tenderloin all over, then rub the meat evenly with oil to coat it thoroughly.
2. In a small bowl, combine chili powder, smoked paprika, garlic powder, salt, and pepper.
3. Rub the spice mixture generously over the tenderloin, ensuring it is well coated.
4. Preheat Zone 1 of the air fryer to 200°C. Place the tenderloin in the basket. Select AIR FRY and cook for 10 minutes. Flip the tenderloin and cook for another 9 to 12 minutes, or until an instant-read thermometer registers at least 64°C. Press START/PAUSE to begin cooking.
5. Remove the tenderloin and let it rest for 5 minutes before slicing. Serve warm and enjoy its bold, smoky flavors.

## Panko Crusted Calf's Liver Strips

**Prep time: 15 minutes | Cook time: 23 to 25 minutes | Serves 4**

- 450 g sliced calf's liver, cut into ½-inch wide strips
- 2 eggs
- 2 tablespoons milk
- 60 g whole wheat flour
- 240 g panko breadcrumbs
- Salt and ground black pepper, to taste
- Cooking spray

1. Preheat Zone 1 to 200°C and spritz the basket with cooking spray.
2. Season the calf's liver strips with salt and ground black pepper on a clean surface.
3. In a large bowl, whisk the eggs with milk. Place the flour in one shallow dish and the panko in another.
4. Dip each liver strip into the flour, then into the egg mixture, and finally coat with panko, shaking off any excess.
5. Arrange half the coated liver strips in a single layer in Zone 1. Spritz with cooking spray.
6. Select AIR FRY, set to 200°C, and cook for 5 minutes, flipping halfway through, until browned. Repeat with the remaining liver strips.
7. Serve immediately and enjoy the crispy, flavorful liver strips!

# Chapter 6
## Fish and Seafood

# Chapter 6 Fish and Seafood

## Crunchy Fish Fingers

**Prep time: 30 minutes | Cook time: 9 minutes | Serves 4**

- 455 g cod fillets
- 85 g finely ground blanched almond flour
- 2 teaspoons Old Bay seasoning
- ½ teaspoon paprika
- Sea salt and freshly ground black pepper, to taste
- 60 ml mayonnaise
- 1 large egg, beaten
- Avocado oil spray
- Tartar sauce, for serving

1. Cut the fish into ¾-inch-wide strips. In a bowl, mix almond flour, Old Bay seasoning, paprika, and salt and pepper. In another bowl, whisk mayonnaise and egg until smooth.
2. Dip each fish strip into the egg mixture, then coat it with the almond flour mixture, pressing gently to ensure it sticks. Place the coated strips on a baking paper-lined tray and freeze for 30 minutes.
3. Spray Zone 1 and Zone 2 with oil. Preheat to 200°C using MATCH. Arrange the fish strips in a single layer in both baskets and spray lightly with oil.
4. Air fry the fish for 5 minutes, flip each piece, spray again, and continue cooking for 4 more minutes, or until golden brown and the internal temperature reaches 60°C.
5. Transfer the fish to a plate and serve hot with tartar sauce.

## Balsamic Tilapia

**Prep time: 5 minutes | Cook time: 15 minutes | Serves 4**

- 4 tilapia fillets, boneless
- 2 tablespoons balsamic vinegar
- 1 teaspoon avocado oil
- 1 teaspoon dried basil

1. Sprinkle the tilapia fillets evenly with balsamic vinegar, avocado oil, and dried basil, ensuring the seasoning is distributed across both sides of the fillets.
2. Lightly spray both Zone 1 and Zone 2 with oil. Preheat to 190°C using MATCH. Once preheated, place the fillets in a single layer in each basket, making sure they do not overlap.
3. Air fry the tilapia fillets at 190°C for 15 minutes. Halfway through cooking, carefully flip the fillets for even browning and crisping.
4. Remove the cooked fillets from the air fryer and serve immediately. Pair with a side of steamed vegetables, rice, or a fresh salad for a complete meal.

## Popcorn Prawns

**Prep time: 15 minutes | Cook time: 18 to 20 minutes | Serves 4**

- 35 g plain flour, plus 2 tablespoons
- ½ teaspoon garlic powder
- 1½ teaspoons Old Bay Seasoning
- ½ teaspoon onion powder
- 120 ml beer, plus 2 tablespoons
- 340 g prawns, peeled and deveined
- Olive oil for misting or cooking spray

Coating:
- 180 g panko crumbs
- 1 teaspoon Old Bay Seasoning
- ½ teaspoon ground black pepper

1. In a large bowl, mix the flour, garlic powder, Old Bay Seasoning, and onion powder. Gradually whisk in the beer until the batter is smooth. Add the prawns and stir to coat them evenly.
2. In a food processor, pulse the coating ingredients until finely crushed. Transfer the crumbs to a shallow dish for easy breading.
3. Preheat both Zone 1 and Zone 2 to 200°C using the MATCH button.
4. Drain the prawns and batter using a colander, stirring gently to remove excess batter. Coat the prawns a handful at a time in the crumbs, ensuring an even layer. Lightly spray the coated prawns with cooking spray.
5. Divide the breaded prawns between Zone 1 and Zone 2, leaving space for airflow. Air fry at 200°C for 5 minutes. Shake both baskets, mist with oil again, and air fry for another 5 minutes. Shake once more, mist lightly, and continue cooking for 3 to 5 minutes until crispy and golden brown.
6. Remove the prawns from the air fryer and serve immediately for the best flavor and crunch.

## Browned Prawns Patties

**Prep time: 15 minutes | Cook time: 10 to 12 minutes | Serves 4**

- 230 g raw prawns, peeled, deveined and chopped finely
- 500 g cooked sushi rice
- 35 g chopped red pepper
- 35 g chopped celery
- 35 g chopped spring onion
- 2 teaspoons Worcestershire sauce
- ½ teaspoon salt
- ½ teaspoon garlic powder
- ½ teaspoon Old Bay seasoning
- 75 g plain bread crumbs
- Cooking spray

1. Preheat both Zone 1 and Zone 2 to 200°C by selecting the MATCH button and pressing START/PAUSE.
2. In a large mixing bowl, combine all the ingredients except the bread crumbs and cooking spray, stirring thoroughly until well incorporated. Scoop out portions of the prawn mixture and shape into 8 equal-sized patties, ensuring each is no more than ½-inch thick. Roll each patty in the bread crumbs, coating evenly, and spray both sides lightly with cooking spray.
3. Divide the patties evenly between Zone 1 and Zone 2, ensuring there is enough space around each for proper air circulation. Select the MATCH button to synchronize the cooking, set the air fryer to 200°C, and air fry for 10 to 12 minutes, flipping the patties halfway through until golden brown and crispy on the outside.
4. Remove the patties from both baskets and divide them among four plates. Serve warm and enjoy immediately.

## Panko Crab Sticks with Mayo Sauce

**Prep time: 5 minutes | Cook time: 12 minutes | Serves 4**

Crab Sticks:
- 2 eggs
- 120 g plain flour
- 50 g panko bread crumbs
- 1 tablespoon Old Bay seasoning
- 455 g crab sticks
- Cooking spray

Mayo Sauce:
- 115 g mayonnaise
- 1 lime, juiced
- 2 garlic cloves, minced

1. Preheat Zone 1 to 200°C. Select Zone 1 and press START/PAUSE to begin preheating.
2. Beat the eggs in a bowl. Place the flour in a shallow dish, and in another shallow dish, mix the panko bread crumbs with Old Bay seasoning until evenly combined.
3. Dredge each crab stick in the flour, shaking off any excess, then dip it into the beaten eggs. Finally, press it into the bread crumb mixture, ensuring an even coating on all sides.
4. Place the crab sticks in Zone 1 of the air fryer, leaving space between them for proper airflow. Lightly spray the sticks with cooking spray. Air fry for 12 minutes, flipping halfway through, until golden brown and crispy.
5. While the crab sticks cook, whisk together the mayo, lime juice, and garlic in a small bowl to prepare the sauce.
6. Serve the crispy crab sticks immediately with the zesty mayo sauce on the side.

## Mouthwatering Cod over Creamy Leek Noodles

**Prep time: 10 minutes | Cook time: 24 minutes | Serves 4**

- 1 small leek, sliced into long thin noodles
- 120 ml double cream
- 2 cloves garlic, minced
- 1 teaspoon fine sea salt, divided
- 4 cod fillets, 110 g each (about 1 inch thick)
- ½ teaspoon ground black pepper

Coating:
- 20 g grated Parmesan cheese
- 2 tablespoons mayonnaise
- 2 tablespoons unsalted butter, softened
- 1 tablespoon chopped fresh thyme, or ½ teaspoon dried thyme leaves, plus more for garnish

1. Preheat Zone 1 and Zone 2 to 200°C. Select the MATCH button and press START/PAUSE to synchronize both zones.
2. In a large bowl, combine all the ingredients except the bread crumbs and cooking spray. Stir the mixture thoroughly until well blended. Shape the mixture into 8 patties of equal size, about ½-inch thick. Coat each patty in bread crumbs on a plate, ensuring an even layer, and spray both sides with cooking spray.
3. Arrange half the patties in Zone 1 and the remaining half in Zone 2, leaving enough space for proper air circulation. Synchronize the cooking with the MATCH button, set to 200°C, and air fry for 10 to 12 minutes. Flip the patties halfway through for even browning until they are golden and crispy.
4. Carefully remove the cooked patties from both zones and divide them among four serving plates. Serve warm while they're still crispy.

## Simple Cheesy Shrimps

**Prep time: 10 minutes | Cook time: 16 minutes | Serves 4 to 6**

- 160 g grated Parmesan cheese
- 4 minced garlic cloves
- 1 teaspoon onion powder
- ½ teaspoon oregano
- 1 teaspoon basil
- 1 teaspoon ground black pepper
- 2 tablespoons olive oil
- 900 g cooked large shrimps, peeled and deveined
- Lemon wedges, for topping
- Cooking spray

1. Preheat the Ninja Double Stack Air Fryer to 180ºC.
2. Lightly spritz both Zone 1 and Zone 2 baskets with cooking spray.
3. In a large bowl, combine all the ingredients except the shrimps. Stir until the mixture is well blended.
4. Dunk the shrimps into the mixture, ensuring they are fully coated, then shake off any excess.
5. Arrange the shrimps in a single layer in the preheated baskets, dividing them evenly between Zone 1 and Zone 2 to avoid overcrowding.
6. Air fry the shrimps for 8 minutes or until they turn opaque, flipping them halfway through cooking for even results.
7. Once cooked, transfer the shrimps to a large plate. Squeeze fresh lemon wedges over the top before serving for added flavor.

## Salmon with Cauliflower

**Prep time: 10 minutes | Cook time: 25 minutes | Serves 4**

- 455 g salmon fillet, diced
- 100 g cauliflower, shredded
- 1 tablespoon dried coriander
- 1 tablespoon coconut oil, melted
- 1 teaspoon ground turmeric
- 60 ml coconut cream

1. In a large bowl, combine the salmon, cauliflower, dried coriander, ground turmeric, coconut cream, and coconut oil. Mix thoroughly to ensure the ingredients are evenly coated.
2. Lightly spray Zone 1 and Zone 2 with oil. Preheat to 180ºC. Once preheated, divide the salmon mixture evenly between the two baskets to avoid overcrowding.
3. Cook at 180ºC for 25 minutes, stirring each basket every 5 minutes to ensure even cooking and prevent burning.
4. Once the salmon mixture is fully cooked and golden, transfer to a serving dish. Serve immediately and enjoy a flavorful, perfectly cooked meal.

## Jalea

**Prep time: 20 minutes | Cook time: 10 minutes | Serves 4**

Salsa Criolla:
- ½ red onion, thinly sliced
- 2 tomatoes, diced
- 1 serrano or red chilli, deseeded and diced
- 1 clove garlic, minced

Fried Seafood:
- 455 g firm, white-fleshed fish such as cod (add an extra 230 g fish if not using prawns)
- 20 large or jumbo prawns, peeled and deveined
- 20 g plain flour
- 20 g cornflour
- 1 teaspoon garlic powder
- 5 g chopped fresh coriander
- Pinch of kosher or coarse sea salt
- 3 limes
- 1 teaspoon kosher or coarse sea salt
- ¼ teaspoon cayenne pepper
- 120 g panko bread crumbs
- 2 eggs, beaten with 2 tablespoons water
- Vegetable oil, for spraying
- Mayonnaise or tartar sauce, for serving (optional)

1. To prepare the Salsa Criolla, combine the red onion, tomatoes, pepper, garlic, coriander, and salt in a medium bowl. Add the juice and zest of two limes, mixing well. Cover and refrigerate while you prepare the seafood to allow the flavors to meld.
2. For the seafood, cut the fish fillets into strips approximately 2 inches long and 1 inch wide. In a shallow dish, mix the flour, cornflour, garlic powder, salt, and cayenne pepper until well blended. Place the panko in a separate dish. Dredge the fish strips in the flour mixture, shaking off any excess. Dip the strips into the egg mixture, ensuring they are fully coated, then dredge them in the panko, pressing gently to adhere. Arrange the prepared fish strips on a plate or rack. Repeat the process for the prawns if included.
3. Lightly spray both Zone 1 and Zone 2 with oil and preheat to 200ºC. Arrange the fish strips and prawns in a single layer in each basket, avoiding overcrowding. Lightly spray the seafood with oil to enhance crispiness. Select MATCH and air fry for 5 minutes. Flip the seafood pieces, then continue air frying for another 4 to 5 minutes, or until golden brown and crispy on the outside, and the fish is opaque and flakes easily.
4. Once the seafood is cooked, transfer it to a platter. Using a slotted spoon, lift the salsa criolla from the bowl, leaving behind any accumulated liquid, and layer it over the fried seafood. Serve immediately with the remaining lime, cut into wedges, alongside mayonnaise or tartar sauce as desired.

# Snapper with Shallot and Tomato & Garlic Prawns

**Prep time: 20 minutes | Cook time: 15 minutes | Serves 2**

### Snapper with Shallot and Tomato | Serves 2

- 2 snapper fillets
- 1 shallot, peeled and sliced
- 2 garlic cloves, halved
- 1 pepper, sliced
- 1 small-sized serrano pepper, sliced
- 1 tomato, sliced
- 1 tablespoon olive oil
- ¼ teaspoon freshly ground black pepper
- ½ teaspoon paprika
- Sea salt, to taste
- 2 bay leaves

### Garlic Prawns | Serves 3

Prawns:

- Olive or vegetable oil, for spraying
- 450 g medium raw prawns, peeled and deveined
- 6 tablespoons unsalted butter, melted

Garlic Butter Sauce:

- 115 g unsalted butter
- 2 teaspoons garlic granules
- 60 g panko bread crumbs
- 2 tablespoons garlic granules
- 1 teaspoon salt
- ½ teaspoon freshly ground black pepper
- ¾ teaspoon salt (omit if using salted butter)

### For Snapper with Shallot and Tomato:

1. Place two sheets of baking paper on a working surface. Lay the fish fillet in the center of one sheet of baking paper.
2. Top the fish with shallot, garlic, peppers, and tomato. Drizzle olive oil over the fish and vegetables, then season with black pepper, paprika, and salt. Add the bay leaves for extra flavor.
3. Fold the other half of the baking paper over the fish. Fold the edges tightly to create a sealed packet, forming a half-moon shape to enclose the fish and vegetables.
4. Preheat the Ninja Double Stack Air Fryer to 200ºC. Press START/PAUSE to begin preheating. Once ready, place the prepared fish packet in Zone 1 of the air fryer.
5. Air fry at 200ºC for 15 minutes. Once cooked, remove from the air fryer and serve warm.

### For Garlic Prawns:

**Make the Prawns:**

1. Preheat the Ninja Double Stack Air Fryer to 200ºC. Line Zone 2 of the air fryer basket with baking paper and spray lightly with oil.
2. Place the prawns and melted butter in a zip-top plastic bag, seal it, and shake well until the prawns are evenly coated with the butter.
3. In a medium bowl, combine the breadcrumbs, garlic, salt, and black pepper. Stir until well mixed.
4. Add the prawns to the breadcrumb mixture and toss until they are evenly coated. Shake off any excess coating.
5. Place the prawns in the prepared air fryer basket in a single layer, making sure they don't overlap. Lightly spray the prawns with oil.
6. Air fry the prawns at 200ºC for 8 to 10 minutes, flipping and spraying them with oil after 4 to 5 minutes, until they are golden brown and crispy.

**Make the Garlic Butter Sauce:**

7. In a microwave-safe bowl, combine the butter, garlic, and salt. Microwave on 50% power for 30 to 60 seconds, stirring every 15 seconds, until the butter is fully melted and the garlic is fragrant.
8. Serve the prawns immediately with the garlic butter sauce on the side for dipping.

# Scallops with Asparagus and Peas

**Prep time: 10 minutes | Cook time: 7 to 10 minutes | Serves 4**

- Cooking oil spray
- 455 g asparagus, ends trimmed, cut into 2-inch pieces
- 100 g sugar snap peas
- 455 g sea scallops
- 1 tablespoon freshly squeezed lemon juice
- 2 teaspoons extra-virgin olive oil
- ½ teaspoon dried thyme
- Salt and freshly ground black pepper, to taste

1. Insert the crisper plate into Zone 1 of the Ninja Double Stack Air Fryer. Preheat the unit to 200ºC.
2. Once preheated, lightly spray the crisper plate with cooking oil. Add the asparagus and sugar snap peas to Zone 1, arranging them evenly.
3. Air fry the vegetables at 200ºC for 10 minutes.
4. While the vegetables cook, inspect the scallops for the small muscle on the side, remove it if present, and discard. In a medium bowl, toss the scallops with lemon juice, olive oil, and thyme. Season generously with salt and pepper.
5. After 3 minutes, check the vegetables—they should just begin to soften. Open Zone 1, place the scallops on top of the vegetables, and reinsert the basket. Cook for another 3 minutes, then remove the basket and shake it gently to mix the contents. Reinsert the basket to continue cooking.
6. When finished, the scallops should feel firm and be opaque in the center, while the vegetables will be tender. Transfer everything to a serving plate and serve immediately.

## Sweet Tilapia Fillets

**Prep time: 5 minutes | Cook time: 14 minutes | Serves 4**

- 2 tablespoons granulated sweetener
- 1 tablespoon apple cider vinegar
- 4 tilapia fillets, boneless
- 1 teaspoon olive oil

1. In a small bowl, whisk together apple cider vinegar, olive oil, and sweetener until well combined.
2. Rub the tilapia fillets evenly with the prepared mixture, ensuring both sides are coated.
3. Preheat the Ninja Double Stack Air Fryer to 180°C. Lightly spray Zone 1 and Zone 2 baskets with oil.
4. Place the tilapia fillets in a single layer in both baskets, dividing them evenly to avoid overcrowding.
5. Air fry the fish at 180°C for 7 minutes on one side. Flip the fillets and cook for an additional 7 minutes, or until the fish is tender and flakes easily with a fork.
6. Remove the tilapia from the air fryer and serve immediately with your choice of sides.

## Lemon Pepper Prawns & Coconut Prawns

**Prep time: 15 minutes | Cook time: 8 minutes**

### Lemon Pepper Prawns | Serves 2

- Olive or vegetable oil, for spraying
- 340 g medium raw prawns, peeled and deveined
- 3 tablespoons lemon juice
- 1 tablespoon olive oil
- 1 teaspoon lemon pepper
- ¼ teaspoon paprika
- ¼ teaspoon granulated garlic

### Coconut Prawns | Serves 2

- Prep time: 5 minutes | Cook time: 6 minutes | Serves 2
- 230 g medium prawns, peeled and deveined
- 2 tablespoons salted butter, melted
- ½ teaspoon Old Bay seasoning
- 25 g desiccated, unsweetened coconut

**For Lemon Pepper Prawns:**

1. Preheat Zone 1 to 200°C. Line the basket with baking paper and lightly coat it with oil spray to prevent sticking.
2. In a medium bowl, mix the prawns with lemon juice, olive oil, lemon pepper, paprika, and minced garlic. Toss thoroughly to ensure the prawns are evenly coated with the seasoning.
3. Arrange the seasoned prawns in the lined basket, spreading them out to allow proper airflow and even cooking.
4. Air fry the prawns for 6 to 8 minutes, shaking the basket halfway through to ensure they cook evenly, until they turn pink, firm, and tender.
5. Serve immediately for the best flavor and freshness.

**For Coconut Prawns:**

1. In a large bowl, toss the prawns with melted butter and Old Bay seasoning until they are evenly coated.
2. Place the desiccated coconut in a separate bowl. Roll each prawn in the coconut, pressing gently to ensure the coating sticks, and arrange them in a single layer in the air fryer basket.
3. Preheat Zone 2 to 200°C. Once preheated, place the basket in Zone 2 and air fry for 6 minutes.
4. Carefully turn the prawns halfway through cooking to ensure even browning. Continue cooking until the prawns are golden and cooked through.
5. Serve immediately while the prawns are hot and crispy for the best taste and texture.

## Pecan-Crusted Catfish

**Prep time: 5 minutes | Cook time: 12 minutes | Serves 4**

- 65 g pecans, finely crushed
- 1 teaspoon fine sea salt
- ¼ teaspoon ground black pepper
- 4 catfish fillets, 110g each

For Garnish (Optional):

- Fresh oregano
- Pecan halves

1. Spray both baskets of the Ninja Double Stack Air Fryer with avocado oil. Preheat to 190°C using the MATCH button and press START/PAUSE for synchronized heating.
2. Mix crushed pecans, salt, and pepper in a bowl. Dredge each catfish fillet in the mixture, pressing the pecans firmly onto both sides. Lightly spray the coated fillets with avocado oil.
3. Place half the fillets in Zone 1 and the rest in Zone 2, leaving space for airflow. Select the MATCH button, set to 190°C, and air fry for 12 minutes, flipping halfway. The fish is done when it flakes easily and is no longer translucent.
4. Carefully remove the fillets and garnish with oregano sprigs and pecan halves, if desired.
5. Store leftovers in an airtight container in the fridge for 3 days. To reheat, preheat the air fryer to 180°C and heat for 4 minutes or until warm.

## Tandoori Prawns

**Prep time: 25 minutes | Cook time: 6 minutes | Serves 4**

- 455 g jumbo raw prawns (21 to 25 count), peeled and deveined
- 1 tablespoon minced fresh ginger
- 3 cloves garlic, minced
- 5 g chopped fresh coriander or parsley, plus more for garnish
- 1 teaspoon ground turmeric
- 1 teaspoon garam masala
- 1 teaspoon smoked paprika
- 1 teaspoon kosher or coarse sea salt
- ½ to 1 teaspoon cayenne pepper
- 2 tablespoons olive oil (for Paleo) or melted ghee
- 2 teaspoons fresh lemon juice

1. In a large bowl, combine the prawns, ginger, garlic, coriander, turmeric, garam masala, paprika, salt, and cayenne. Toss thoroughly to coat the prawns evenly. Add the oil or ghee and toss again to ensure a light coating. Let the prawns marinate at room temperature for 15 minutes, or cover and refrigerate for up to 8 hours.
2. Lightly spray both Zone 1 and Zone 2 baskets with oil. Place the prawns in a single layer across both baskets, avoiding overcrowding. Preheat the air fryer to 160ºC, then press START/PAUSE to begin cooking. Air fry the prawns for 6 minutes.
3. Once cooking is complete, transfer the prawns to a serving platter. Cover and let them rest for about 5 minutes to finish cooking in the residual heat.
4. Sprinkle the prawns with lemon juice and toss gently to coat. Garnish with additional fresh coriander and serve immediately.

## Salmon Spring Rolls

**Prep time: 20 minutes | Cook time: 8 to 10 minutes | Serves 4**

- 230 g salmon fillet
- 1 teaspoon toasted sesame oil
- 1 onion, sliced
- 8 rice paper wrappers
- 1 yellow pepper, thinly sliced
- 1 carrot, shredded
- 10 g chopped fresh flat-leaf parsley
- 15 g chopped fresh basil

1. Place the salmon in Zone 1 of the Ninja Double Stack Air Fryer basket and drizzle it with sesame oil. Add the sliced onion, spreading it evenly around the salmon. Preheat the air fryer to 190ºC and press START/PAUSE to begin cooking. Air fry for 8 to 10 minutes, or until the salmon flakes easily with a fork and the onion becomes tender.
2. While the salmon cooks, fill a small shallow bowl with warm water. One at a time, dip the rice paper wrappers into the water and lay them flat on a clean work surface.
3. Once the salmon and onion are ready, divide them into eight portions. Top each rice paper wrapper with one-eighth of the salmon and onion mixture, yellow pepper strips, shredded carrot, parsley, and basil. Roll each wrapper tightly, folding in the sides to secure the filling.
4. If desired, place the rolls back into Zone 1 and Zone 2 of the air fryer in a single layer. Preheat to 190ºC and press START/PAUSE to begin cooking. Air fry for 7 to 9 minutes, or until the rolls are golden and crunchy.
5. Remove the rolls from the air fryer and let them cool slightly. Slice each roll in half and serve immediately.

## Sea Bass with Potato Scales

**Prep time: 10 minutes | Cook time: 10 minutes | Serves 2**

- 2 fillets of sea bass, 170- to 230 g each
- Salt and freshly ground black pepper, to taste
- 60 ml mayonnaise
- 2 teaspoons finely chopped lemon zest
- 1 teaspoon chopped fresh thyme
- 2 Fingerling, or new potatoes, very thinly sliced into rounds
- Olive oil
- ½ clove garlic, crushed into a paste
- 1 tablespoon capers, drained and rinsed
- 1 tablespoon olive oil
- 1 teaspoon lemon juice, to taste

1. Preheat the Ninja Double Stack Air Fryer to 200ºC.
2. Season the fish fillets generously with salt and freshly ground black pepper. In a small bowl, mix mayonnaise, lemon zest, and thyme until smooth. Spread a thin layer of the mayonnaise mixture over both sides of the fillets. Arrange potato slices in overlapping rows on top of the fish, simulating fish scales. To help the potato slices stick, dab a bit more mayonnaise along the edge of each row before adding the next. Gently press the potato slices onto the fish to secure them, then season the potato layer with salt and brush or spray with olive oil.
3. Place the prepared fish fillets in a single layer in Zone 1 and Zone 2 baskets. Air fry at 200ºC for 8 to 10 minutes, depending on the thickness of the fillets. For fillets 1 inch thick, cook for 10 minutes.
4. While the fish cooks, prepare the caper aïoli by mixing the remaining mayonnaise mixture with garlic, capers, olive oil, and lemon juice in a small bowl.
5. Once cooked, the potato layer should be golden and crispy, and the fish should flake easily. Serve the fish warm with a dollop of the caper aïoli on top or on the side.

## Marinated Salmon Fillets

**Prep time: 10 minutes | Cook time: 15 to 20 minutes | Serves 4**

- 60 ml soy sauce
- 60 ml rice wine vinegar
- 1 tablespoon brown sugar
- 1 tablespoon olive oil
- 1 teaspoon mustard powder
- 1 teaspoon ground ginger
- ½ teaspoon freshly ground black pepper
- ½ teaspoon minced garlic
- 4 salmon fillets, 170 g each, skin-on
- Cooking spray

1. In a small bowl, mix soy sauce, rice wine vinegar, brown sugar, olive oil, mustard powder, ginger, black pepper, and garlic to create a marinade.
2. Place the fish fillets in a shallow dish and pour the marinade over them. Cover and refrigerate for at least 1 hour, turning the fillets occasionally to ensure they are evenly coated.
3. Preheat the Ninja Double Stack Air Fryer to 190ºC. Lightly spray both Zone 1 and Zone 2 baskets with cooking spray, then press START/PAUSE to begin preheating.
4. Remove the fillets from the marinade, shaking off any excess, and place them skin-side down in a single layer in the baskets. If needed, divide the fillets between Zone 1 and Zone 2 to avoid overcrowding.
5. Air fry at 190ºC for 15 to 20 minutes, or until the thickest part of the fillets reaches an internal temperature of 64ºC. The fillets should be cooked through and flaky.
6. Transfer the cooked fillets to a serving platter and serve hot.

## Coconut Prawns with Pineapple-Lemon Sauce

**Prep time: 10 minutes | Cook time: 18 minutes | Serves 4**

- 60 g light brown sugar
- 2 teaspoons cornflour
- ⅛ teaspoon plus ½ teaspoon salt, divided
- 110 g crushed pineapple with syrup
- 2 tablespoons freshly squeezed lemon juice
- 1 tablespoon yellow mustard
- 680 g raw large prawns, peeled and deveined
- 2 eggs
- 30 g plain flour
- 95 g desiccated, unsweetened coconut
- ¼ teaspoon garlic granules
- Olive oil spray

1. In a medium saucepan over medium heat, combine the brown sugar, cornflour, and ⅛ teaspoon of salt. Stir well.
2. As the brown sugar mixture melts, stir in the crushed pineapple with syrup, lemon juice, and mustard. Cook for about 4 minutes, allowing the mixture to thicken and begin to boil. Let it boil for 1 minute. Remove the pan from heat and set it aside to cool while you prepare the prawns.
3. Place the prawns on a plate and pat them dry with paper towels.
4. In a small bowl, whisk the eggs until smooth.
5. In a medium bowl, combine the flour, desiccated coconut, the remaining ½ teaspoon of salt, and garlic granules. Stir well to mix the dry ingredients.
6. Insert the crisper plate into Zone 1 of the Ninja Double Stack Air Fryer basket, then insert the basket into the unit. Preheat the unit to 200ºC by selecting the desired temperature, then press START/PAUSE to begin preheating.
7. Dip each prawn into the egg mixture, then coat them in the coconut mixture, pressing lightly to ensure they are well coated.
8. Once preheated, place a baking paper liner into the basket and arrange the coated prawns in a single layer on the liner. Lightly spray the prawns with olive oil.
9. Air fry the prawns for 6 minutes, then carefully remove the basket, flip the prawns, and spray them with more olive oil. Reinsert the basket into Zone 1 or Zone 2, depending on which zone you are using, and resume cooking. Check the prawns after 3 more minutes. If they are browned, they are done. If not, continue cooking for additional time.
10. Once the prawns are cooked, transfer them to a serving platter and serve with the prepared pineapple sauce.

## Crab-Stuffed Avocado Boats

**Prep time: 5 minutes | Cook time: 7 minutes | Serves 4**

- 2 medium avocados, halved and pitted
- 230 g cooked crab meat
- ¼ teaspoon Old Bay seasoning
- 2 tablespoons peeled and diced brown onion
- 2 tablespoons mayonnaise

1. Scoop out the flesh from each avocado half, leaving about ½ inch around the edges to form a shell. Chop the scooped-out avocado into small pieces.
2. In a medium bowl, combine the crab meat, Old Bay seasoning, onion, mayonnaise, and chopped avocado. Mix until well combined. Spoon ¼ of the mixture into each avocado shell.
3. Preheat the Ninja Double Stack Air Fryer to 180ºC by selecting the temperature and pressing START/PAUSE to begin. Place the filled avocado boats into the air fryer basket.
4. Air fry at 180ºC for 7 minutes. The tops of the avocados should be browned, and the mixture should be bubbling when done.
5. Carefully remove the avocado boats from the air fryer and serve warm.

## Crab Cakes & White Fish with Cauliflower

**Prep time: 30 minutes | Cook time: 13 minutes | Serves 4**

### Crab Cakes | Serves 4

- 2 tins lump crab meat, 170 g each
- ¼ cup blanched finely ground almond flour
- 1 large egg
- 2 tablespoons full-fat mayonnaise
- ½ teaspoon Dijon mustard
- ½ tablespoon lemon juice
- ½ medium green pepper, seeded and chopped
- 235 g chopped spring onion
- ½ teaspoon Old Bay seasoning

### White Fish with Cauliflower | Serves 4

- 230 g cauliflower florets
- ½ teaspoon English mustard
- 2 tablespoons butter, room temperature
- ½ tablespoon coriander, minced
- 2 tablespoons sour cream
- 340 g cooked white fish
- Salt and freshly cracked black pepper, to taste

**For Crab Cakes:**

1. In a large bowl, combine all ingredients and mix well. Form the mixture into four balls, then flatten them into patties.
2. Preheat the Ninja Double Stack Air Fryer to 180°C by selecting the temperature and pressing START/PAUSE to begin. Once preheated, place the patties in a single layer in Zone 1 or of the air fryer basket.
3. Air fry at 180°C for 10 minutes, flipping the patties halfway through the cooking time for even browning.
4. Once cooked, serve the patties warm.

**For White Fish with Cauliflower:**

1. Boil the cauliflower until tender. Once cooked, purée the cauliflower in a blender and transfer it to a mixing bowl.
2. Stir in the fish, coriander, salt, and black pepper, mixing well until evenly combined.
3. Add the sour cream, English mustard, and butter to the mixture, stirring until everything is well incorporated. Using your hands, shape the mixture into patties.
4. Place the patties in the refrigerator and let them chill for about 2 hours.
5. Preheat the Ninja Double Stack Air Fryer to 200°C by selecting the temperature and pressing START/PAUSE to begin. Once preheated, place the patties in a single layer in Zone 2 of the air fryer basket.
6. Air fry at 200°C for 13 minutes, flipping halfway through for even cooking.

## Baked Grouper with Tomatoes and Garlic & Crab Cakes with Peppers

**Prep time: 5 minutes | Cook time: 12 minutes**

### Baked Grouper with Tomatoes and Garlic | Serves 4

- 4 grouper fillets
- ½ teaspoon salt
- 3 garlic cloves, minced
- 1 tomato, sliced
- 45 g sliced Kalamata olives
- 10 g fresh dill, roughly chopped
- Juice of 1 lemon
- ¼ cup olive oil

### Crab Cakes with Peppers | Serves 4

- 230 g jumbo lump crab meat
- 1 egg, beaten
- Juice of ½ lemon
- 50 g bread crumbs
- 35 g diced green pepper
- 35 g diced red pepper
- 60 g mayonnaise
- 1 tablespoon Old Bay seasoning
- 1 teaspoon plain flour
- Cooking spray

**For Baked Grouper with Tomatoes and Garlic:**

1. Preheat the Ninja Double Stack Air Fryer to 190°C by selecting the temperature and pressing START/PAUSE to begin.
2. Season the grouper fillets on all sides with salt. Place the fillets in Zone 1 of the air fryer basket and top with the minced garlic, tomato slices, olives, and fresh dill.
3. Drizzle the lemon juice and olive oil over the top of the grouper fillets. Air fry at 190°C for 10 to 12 minutes, or until the internal temperature reaches 64°C and the fish flakes easily.

**For Crab Cakes with Peppers:**

1. Preheat the Ninja Double Stack Air Fryer to 190°C by selecting the temperature and pressing START/PAUSE to begin.
2. Make the crab cakes: In a large bowl, combine all ingredients except the flour and oil. Stir until everything is well incorporated.
3. Divide the crab mixture into four equal portions and shape each portion into a patty using your hands. Sprinkle each patty with ¼ teaspoon of flour on top.
4. Arrange the crab cakes in a single layer in Zone 2 of the air fryer basket and lightly spritz with cooking spray.
5. Air fry at 190°C for 10 minutes, flipping the crab cakes halfway through, or until they are cooked through and golden brown.
6. Once done, divide the crab cakes among four plates and serve immediately.

## Classic Prawns Empanadas

**Prep time: 10 minutes | Cook time: 8 minutes | Serves 5**

- 230 g raw prawns, peeled, deveined and chopped
- 1 small chopped red onion
- 1 spring onion, chopped
- 2 garlic cloves, minced
- 2 tablespoons minced red pepper
- 2 tablespoons chopped fresh coriander
- ½ tablespoon fresh lime juice
- ¼ teaspoon sweet paprika
- ⅛ teaspoon kosher salt
- ⅛ teaspoon crushed red pepper flakes (optional)
- 1 large egg, beaten
- 10 frozen Goya Empanada Discos, thawed
- Cooking spray

1. In a medium bowl, mix the prawns, red onion, spring onion, garlic, pepper, coriander, lime juice, paprika, salt, and pepper flakes (if using) until well combined.
2. In a small bowl, beat the egg with 1 teaspoon of water to create a smooth egg wash.
3. Place an empanada disc on a flat work surface. Spoon 2 tablespoons of the prawn mixture into the center of the disc. Brush the outer edges with the egg wash, then fold the disc over to form a half-moon shape. Gently press the edges to seal, then crimp the edges with a fork for a secure seal. Brush the tops of the empanadas with the remaining egg wash.
4. Preheat the Ninja Double Stack Air Fryer to 190°C.
5. Lightly spray the bottom of both Zone 1 and Zone 2 baskets with cooking spray to prevent sticking. Working in batches if needed, arrange the empanadas in a single layer in each basket. Air fry at 190°C for 8 minutes, flipping halfway through, until golden brown and crispy.
6. Transfer the empanadas to a serving plate and serve hot.

## Prawns Scampi

**Prep time: 8 minutes | Cook time: 8 minutes | Serves 4**

- 4 tablespoons salted butter or ghee
- 1 tablespoon fresh lemon juice
- 1 tablespoon minced garlic
- 2 teaspoons red pepper flakes
- 455 g prawns (21 to 25 count), peeled and deveined
- 2 tablespoons dry white wine or chicken broth
- 2 tablespoons chopped fresh basil, plus more for sprinkling, or 1 teaspoon dried
- 1 tablespoon chopped fresh chives, or 1 teaspoon dried

1. Place a baking pan into Zone 1 of the Ninja Double Stack Air Fryer. Preheat to 160°C for 8 minutes to warm the pan, ensuring the butter will melt quickly.
2. Carefully remove the pan from Zone 1 and add the butter, lemon juice, garlic, and red pepper flakes. Return the pan to the air fryer.
3. Cook at 160°C for 2 minutes, stirring once to ensure the garlic infuses the butter. This step is crucial for creating the rich garlic flavor.
4. Remove the pan and add the prawns, broth, basil, and chives. Gently stir to combine all ingredients evenly.
5. Place the pan back into Zone 1 and cook at 160°C for 5 minutes, stirring once halfway through to ensure even cooking.
6. Once cooked, remove the pan and stir the prawn mixture thoroughly. Let it rest for 1 minute on a wire rack, allowing the residual heat to finish cooking the prawns without overcooking.
7. Stir once more, sprinkle with additional fresh basil, and serve immediately.

# Salmon on Bed of Fennel and Carrot & Cornmeal-Crusted Trout Fingers

**Prep time: 15 minutes | Cook time: 13 to 14 minutes | Serves 2**

### Salmon on Bend of Fennel | Serves 2

- 1 fennel bulb, thinly sliced
- 1 large carrot, peeled and sliced
- 1 small onion, thinly sliced

### Cornmeal-Crusted Trout Fingers | Serves 2

- 70 g yellow cornmeal, medium or finely ground (not coarse)
- 20 g plain flour
- 1½ teaspoons baking powder
- 1 teaspoon kosher or coarse sea salt, plus more as needed
- ½ teaspoon freshly ground black pepper, plus more as needed
- ⅛ teaspoon cayenne pepper
- 340 g skinless trout fillets, cut into strips 1 inch wide and 3 inches long
- 60 ml low-fat sour cream
- ¼ teaspoon coarsely ground pepper
- 2 salmon fillets, 140 g each
- 3 large eggs, lightly beaten
- Cooking spray
- 115 g mayonnaise
- 2 tablespoons capers, rinsed and finely chopped
- 1 tablespoon fresh tarragon
- 1 teaspoon fresh lemon juice, plus lemon wedges, for serving

### For Salmon on Bed of Fennel and Carrot:

1. Combine the fennel, carrot, and onion in a bowl and toss until well mixed.
2. Transfer the vegetable mixture into a baking pan. Preheat the Ninja Double Stack Air Fryer to 200°C by selecting the temperature and pressing START/PAUSE. Once preheated, place the baking pan into Zone 1. Roast the vegetables for 4 minutes or until they are crisp-tender.
3. Carefully remove the pan from the air fryer. Stir in the sour cream and sprinkle the vegetables with pepper to taste.
4. Place the salmon fillets on top of the vegetable mixture in the pan.
5. Return the pan to the air fryer and roast for another 9 to 10 minutes, or until the salmon flakes easily when tested with a fork.

### For Cornmeal-Crusted Trout Fingers:

1. Preheat the Ninja Double Stack Air Fryer to 200°C by selecting the temperature and pressing START/PAUSE to begin.
2. In a large bowl, whisk together the cornmeal, flour, baking powder, salt, black pepper, and cayenne. Dip the trout strips in the egg, then toss them in the cornmeal mixture until fully coated. Place the coated trout strips on a rack set over a baking sheet and spray generously with cooking spray.
3. Transfer half of the coated trout strips to Zone 2 of the air fryer. Air fry at 200°C for about 6 minutes, or until the fish is golden brown and cooked through. Once done, transfer the trout fingers to a plate and repeat with the remaining fish in the second zone.
4. Meanwhile, in a small bowl, whisk together the mayonnaise, capers, tarragon, and lemon juice. Season the tartar sauce with salt and black pepper to taste.
5. Serve the hot trout fingers with the tartar sauce and lemon wedges on the side.

# Chapter 7
# Snacks and Starters

# Chapter 7 Snacks and Starters

## Taco-Spiced Chickpeas & Carrot Chips

**Prep time: 5 minutes | Cook time: 17 minutes**

**Taco-Spiced Chickpeas | Serves 3**

- Oil, for spraying
- 1 (439 g) tin chickpeas, drained

**1 teaspoon chilli powder**

- ½ teaspoon cumin powder
- ½ teaspoon salt
- ½ teaspoon garlic powder
- 2 teaspoons lime juice

**Carrot Chips | Serves 4**

- 1 tablespoon olive oil, plus more for greasing the basket
- 4 to 5 medium carrots, trimmed and thinly sliced
- 1 teaspoon seasoned salt

**For Taco-Spiced Chickpeas:**

1. Line the air fryer basket with baking paper and lightly spray it with oil. Place the chickpeas in the prepared basket, spreading them out in an even layer.
2. Preheat the Zone 1 of Ninja Double Stack Air Fryer to 200°C by selecting the temperature and pressing START/PAUSE to begin. Once preheated, air fry the chickpeas for 17 minutes, shaking or stirring the chickpeas every 5 to 7 minutes and spraying lightly with oil each time.
3. In a small bowl, mix together the chili powder, cumin, salt, and garlic.
4. When 2 to 3 minutes of cooking time remain, sprinkle half of the seasoning mix over the chickpeas and continue cooking until done.
5. Transfer the chickpeas to a medium-sized bowl and toss with the remaining seasoning mix and lime juice. Serve immediately.

**For Carrot Chips:**

1. Preheat Zone 2 of the air fryer to 200°C. Grease the air fryer basket with the olive oil. 2. Toss the carrot slices with 1 tablespoon of olive oil and salt in a medium-sized bowl until thoroughly coated. 3. Arrange the carrot slices in the greased basket. You may need to work in batches to avoid overcrowding. 4. Air fry for 8 to 10 minutes until the carrot slices are crisp-tender. Shake the basket once during cooking. 5. Transfer the carrot slices to a bowl and repeat with the remaining carrots. 6. Allow to cool for 5 minutes and serve.

## Classic Poutine

**Prep time: 15 minutes | Cook time: 25 minutes | Serves 2**

- 2 russet or Maris Piper potatoes, scrubbed and cut into ½-inch sticks
- 2 teaspoons vegetable oil
- 2 tablespoons butter
- ¼ onion, minced
- ¼ teaspoon dried thyme
- 1 clove garlic, smashed
- 3 tablespoons plain flour
- 1 teaspoon tomato paste
- 350 ml beef stock
- 2 teaspoons Worcestershire sauce
- Salt and freshly ground black pepper, to taste
- 160 g chopped string cheese

1. Bring a pot of water to a boil. Add the potato sticks and blanch for 4 minutes.
2. Preheat the Ninja Double Stack Air Fryer to 200°C by selecting the temperature and pressing START/PAUSE to begin.
3. Drain the potato sticks and rinse them under cold running water. Pat the sticks dry with paper towels to remove any excess moisture.
4. Transfer the dried potato sticks to a large bowl and drizzle with vegetable oil. Toss well to coat evenly.
5. Place the potato sticks in Zone 1 and Zone 2 of the air fryer basket, making sure they are spread evenly without overcrowding.
6. Air fry the potato sticks at 200°C for 25 minutes, or until golden brown and crispy. Shake the baskets at least three times during the cooking process to ensure even frying.
7. Meanwhile, prepare the gravy: Heat the butter in a saucepan over medium heat until melted.
8. Add the onion, thyme, and garlic to the saucepan and sauté for 5 minutes, or until the onion is translucent.
9. Add the flour and sauté for an additional 2 minutes, stirring to prevent lumps.
10. Pour in the tomato paste and beef stock, then cook for 1 more minute, or until the gravy thickens slightly.
11. Drizzle in the Worcestershire sauce, then sprinkle with salt and ground black pepper to taste.
12. Reduce the heat to low to keep the gravy warm until ready to serve.
13. Once the fries are cooked, transfer the fried potato sticks to a plate. Sprinkle them with salt and ground black pepper.
14. Scatter string cheese over the fries and pour the warm gravy over them.
15. Serve the fries immediately while they are hot.

## Easy Roasted Chickpeas

**Prep time: 5 minutes | Cook time: 15 minutes | Makes about 240 ml**

- 1 (425 g) tin chickpeas, drained
- 2 teaspoons curry powder
- ¼ teaspoon salt
- 1 tablespoon olive oil

1. Drain the chickpeas thoroughly and spread them in a single layer on kitchen roll. Cover with another paper towel and press gently to remove any excess moisture. Be careful not to press too hard, as this could crush the chickpeas.
2. In a small bowl, mix the curry powder and salt together.
3. Place the drained chickpeas in a medium-sized bowl and sprinkle with the seasoning mixture. Stir well to coat the chickpeas evenly.
4. Add the olive oil to the chickpeas and stir again to ensure the oil is well distributed.
5. Preheat the Ninja Double Stack Air Fryer to 200°C by selecting the temperature and pressing START/PAUSE to begin. Once preheated, place the chickpeas in Zone 1 and Zone 2 of the air fryer baskets in a single layer, ensuring even cooking. Air fry at 200°C for 15 minutes, shaking the baskets halfway through cooking for even crisping.
6. Once cooked, remove the chickpeas and allow them to cool completely. Transfer to an airtight container for storage.

## Soft white cheese Stuffed Jalapeño Chillies Poppers

**Prep time: 12 minutes | Cook time: 6 to 8 minutes | Serves 10**

- 227 g soft white cheese, at room temperature
- 80 g panko breadcrumbs, divided
- 2 tablespoons fresh parsley, minced
- 1 teaspoon chilli powder
- 10 jalapeño chillies chillies, halved and seeded
- Cooking oil spray

1. In a small bowl, whisk together the soft white cheese, 40g of panko, parsley, and chili powder until fully combined. Stuff the cheese mixture into the halved jalapeños.
2. Sprinkle the tops of the stuffed jalapeños with the remaining 40g of panko and gently press it into the filling.
3. Preheat the Ninja Double Stack Air Fryer by selecting the AIR FRY function, setting the temperature to 190°C, and the time to 3 minutes. Press START/PAUSE to begin.
4. Once the unit is preheated, spray the crisper plate with cooking oil. Place the stuffed jalapeño poppers in Zone 1 and Zone 2 of the air fryer basket, ensuring they are in a single layer.
5. Set the air fryer to AIR FRY at 190°C for 8 minutes. Press START/PAUSE to begin cooking.
6. After 6 minutes, check the poppers. If they are softened and the cheese is melted, they are ready. If not, continue cooking for additional time.
7. Once cooked, remove the poppers from the air fryer and serve warm.

## Crispy Green Bean Fries with Lemon-Yoghurt Sauce

**Prep time: 5 minutes | Cook time: 5 minutes | Serves 4**

French beans:
- 1 egg
- 2 tablespoons water
- 1 tablespoon wholemeal flour
- ¼ teaspoon paprika
- ½ teaspoon garlic powder
- ½ teaspoon salt
- 25 g wholemeal breadcrumbs
- 227 g whole French beans

Lemon-Yoghurt Sauce:
- 120 ml non-fat plain Greek yoghurt
- 1 tablespoon lemon juice
- ¼ teaspoon salt
- ⅛ teaspoon cayenne pepper

**Make the French Beans:**

1. Preheat the Ninja Double Stack Air Fryer to 190°C by selecting the temperature and pressing START/PAUSE to begin.
2. In a medium shallow dish, beat the egg and water together until frothy.
3. In a separate medium shallow dish, whisk together the flour, paprika, garlic powder, and salt. Then, mix in the breadcrumbs until well combined.
4. Lightly spray the bottom of both Zone 1 and Zone 2 baskets with cooking spray.
5. Dip each green bean into the egg mixture, then into the breadcrumb mixture, coating the outside with crumbs. Arrange the French beans in a single layer in Zone 1 and Zone 2 of the air fryer basket, ensuring they don't overlap for even cooking.
6. Air fry the French beans at 190°C for 5 minutes, or until the breading is golden and crispy. Shake the baskets halfway through cooking for even crisping.

**Make the Lemon-Yogurt Sauce:**

7. In a small bowl, combine the yogurt, lemon juice, salt, and cayenne pepper. Stir until smooth and well mixed.
8. Serve the crispy green bean fries alongside the lemon-yogurt sauce as a tasty snack or starter.

# Black Bean Maize Dip & Air Fried Pot Stickers

**Prep time: 10 minutes | Cook time: 18 to 20 minutes**

### Black Bean Maize Dip | Serves 4

- ½ (425 g) tin black beans, drained and rinsed
- ½ (425 g) tin sweetcorn, drained and rinsed
- 60 g chunky salsa
- 57 g low-fat soft white cheese
- 40 g shredded low-fat Cheddar cheese
- ½ teaspoon cumin powder
- ½ teaspoon paprika
- Salt and freshly ground black pepper, to taste

### Air Fried Pot Stickers | Makes 30 pot stickers

- 35 g finely chopped cabbage
- 30 g finely chopped red pepper
- 2 spring onions, finely chopped
- 1 egg, beaten
- 2 tablespoons cocktail sauce
- 2 teaspoons low-salt soy sauce
- 30 wonton wrappers
- 1 tablespoon water, for brushing the wrappers

### For Black Bean Maize Dip:

1. Preheat the Ninja Double Stack Air Fryer to 160°C by selecting the temperature and pressing START/PAUSE to begin.
2. In a medium-sized bowl, combine the black beans, sweetcorn, salsa, soft white cheese, Cheddar cheese, cumin, and paprika. Season with salt and pepper to taste and stir until everything is well combined.
3. Spoon the mixture into a baking dish that fits in the air fryer basket.
4. Place the baking dish in Zone 1 of the air fryer basket and air fry for about 10 minutes, or until the mixture is heated through.
5. Serve hot.

### For Air Fried Pot Stickers:

1. Preheat the Ninja Double Stack Air Fryer to 180°C by selecting the temperature and pressing START/PAUSE to begin.
2. In a small bowl, combine the cabbage, pepper, spring onions, egg, cocktail sauce, and soy sauce. Mix well until everything is evenly combined.
3. Place about 1 teaspoon of the mixture in the center of each wonton wrapper. Fold the wrapper in half to cover the filling, dampen the edges with water, and seal the wrapper. Crimp the edges with your fingers to form the shape of pot stickers, if desired. Lightly brush the wrappers with water to help seal them.
4. Place the pot stickers Zone 2 of the air fryer basket, ensuring they are in a single layer with space in between. You may need to work in batches. Air fry at 180°C for 9 to 10 minutes, or until the pot stickers are hot and the bottoms are lightly browned.
5. Once cooked, serve the pot stickers hot.

# Prawns Egg Rolls

**Prep time: 15 minutes | Cook time: 10 minutes per batch | Serves 4**

- 1 tablespoon mixed vegetables oil
- ½ head green or savoy cabbage, finely shredded
- 90 g grated carrots
- 240 ml canned bean sprouts, drained
- 1 tablespoon soy sauce
- ½ teaspoon sugar
- 1 teaspoon sesame oil
- 60 ml hoisin sauce
- Freshly ground black pepper, to taste
- 454 g cooked prawns, diced
- 30 g spring onions
- 8 egg roll wrappers (or use spring roll pastry)
- mixed vegetables oil
- Duck sauce

1. Preheat a large sauté pan over medium-high heat. Add the oil and cook the cabbage, carrots, and bean sprouts until they start to wilt, about 3 minutes. Add the soy sauce, sugar, sesame oil, hoisin sauce, and black pepper. Sauté for a few more minutes. Stir in the prawns and spring onions and cook until the mixed vegetables are just tender. Transfer the mixture to a colander over a bowl to cool. Press or squeeze out any excess water from the filling to avoid soggy egg rolls.
2. Make the egg rolls: Place the egg roll wrappers on a flat surface with one of the points facing towards you, making them look like diamonds. Divide the filling evenly between the eight wrappers. Spoon the mixture into the center of each wrapper. Spread the filling across the center of the wrapper from left corner to right corner, leaving 2 inches from each corner empty. Brush the empty sides of the wrapper with a little water. Fold the bottom corner tightly over the filling, avoiding air pockets. Fold in the left and right corners toward the center. Then, tightly roll the egg roll from the bottom to the top open corner. Press to seal the egg roll, brushing with a little extra water if needed. Repeat with all 8 egg rolls.
3. Preheat the Ninja Double Stack Air Fryer to 190°C by selecting the temperature and pressing START/PAUSE to begin.
4. Spray or brush all sides of the egg rolls with vegetable oil. Place four egg rolls in Zone 1 and Zone 2 of the air fryer basket. Air fry at 190°C for 10 minutes, turning them over halfway through the cooking time for even browning.
5. Once cooked, serve the egg rolls hot with duck sauce or your favorite dipping sauce.

## Spiralized Potato Nest with Tomato Tomato Ketchup & Crispy Mozzarella Cheese Sticks

**Prep time: 10 minutes | Cook time: 15 minutes**

### Spiralized Potato Nest with Tomato Tomato Ketchup | Serves 2

- 1 large russet potatoes or Maris Piper potato (about 340 g)
- 2 tablespoons mixed vegetables oil
- 1 tablespoon hot smoked paprika
- ½ teaspoon garlic powder
- Rock salt and freshly ground black pepper, to taste
- 120 ml canned chopped tomatoes
- 2 tablespoons apple cider vinegar
- 1 tablespoon dark brown sugar
- 1 tablespoon Worcestershire sauce
- 1 teaspoon mild hot sauce

### Crispy Mozzarella Cheese Sticks | Serves 4

- 65 g plain flour
- 1 egg, beaten
- 25 g panko breadcrumbs
- 30 g grated Parmesan cheese
- 1 teaspoon Italian seasoning
- ½ teaspoon garlic salt
- 6 mozzarella cheese sticks, halved crosswise
- Olive oil spray

**For Spiralized Potato Nest with Tomato Tomato**

1. Using a spiralizer, spiralize the potato, then place it in a large colander. (If you don't have a spiralizer, cut the potato into thin ⅛-inch-thick matchsticks.) Rinse the potatoes under cold running water until the water runs clear. Spread the potatoes out on a double layer of kitchen roll and pat them completely dry.
2. In a large bowl, combine the potatoes, oil, paprika, and garlic powder. Season with salt and pepper to taste, and toss to coat the potatoes evenly.
3. Preheat the Ninja Double Stack Air Fryer to 200ºC by selecting the temperature and pressing START/PAUSE to begin. Once preheated, transfer the potatoes to Zone 1 of the air fryer baskets in a single layer, ensuring enough space for air circulation. Air fry at 200ºC for 15 minutes, shaking the baskets halfway through for even crisping.
4. Meanwhile, in a small blender, purée the tomatoes, vinegar, brown sugar, Worcestershire sauce, and hot sauce until smooth. Pour the mixture into a small saucepan or frying pan and simmer over medium heat for 3 to 5 minutes until it reduces by half. Transfer the homemade tomato ketchup into a bowl and let it cool.
5. Once the spiralized potato nests are golden brown and crisp, remove them from the air fryer and serve hot with the homemade tomato ketchup.

**For Crispy Mozzarella Cheese Sticks:**

1. Put the flour in a small bowl.
2. Put the beaten egg in another small bowl.
3. In a medium-sized bowl, stir together the panko, Parmesan cheese, Italian seasoning, and garlic salt.
4. Roll each mozzarella cheese stick half in the flour, dip it into the egg, and then roll it in the panko mixture to coat. Press the coating lightly to make sure the breadcrumbs stick to the cheese. Repeat with the remaining 11 mozzarella cheese sticks.
5. Preheat the Ninja Double Stack Air Fryer by selecting the AIR FRY function, setting the temperature to 200ºC, and the time to 3 minutes. Press START/PAUSE to begin preheating.
6. Once the unit is preheated, spray the crisper plate with olive oil. Place a baking paper liner in Zone 2 of the air fryer basket. Arrange the mozzarella cheese sticks in a single layer, ensuring they don't touch. Lightly spray the sticks with olive oil.
7. Select AIR FRY, set the temperature to 200ºC, and set the time to 5 minutes. Press START/PAUSE to begin cooking.
8. Once cooking is complete, the mozzarella cheese sticks should be golden and crispy. Let them stand for 1 minute before transferring them to a serving plate. Serve warm.

## Crunchy Tex-Mex Tortilla Chips

**Prep time: 5 minutes | Cook time: 5 minutes | Serves 4**

- Olive oil
- ½ teaspoon salt
- ½ teaspoon cumin powder
- ½ teaspoon chili powder
- ½ teaspoon paprika
- Pinch cayenne pepper
- 8 (6-inch) sweetcorn tortillas, each cut into 6 wedges

1. Lightly spray the air fryer basket in Zone 1 and Zone 2 with olive oil.
2. In a small bowl, combine the salt, cumin, chili powder, paprika, and cayenne pepper.
3. Arrange the tortilla wedges in a single layer in Zone 1 and Zone 2 of the air fryer basket. Spray the tortillas lightly with olive oil and sprinkle with some of the seasoning mixture. You will need to cook the tortillas in batches to avoid overcrowding.
4. Preheat the Ninja Double Stack Air Fryer to 190ºC by selecting the temperature and pressing START/PAUSE to begin. Once preheated, air fry the tortillas for 2 to 3 minutes. Shake the baskets and cook for an additional 2 to 3 minutes, or until the chips are light brown and crispy.
5. Watch the chips closely to ensure they do not burn. Once crispy, remove from the air fryer and serve warm.

# Cinnamon-Apple Crisps & Kale Crisps with Tex-Mex Dip

**Prep time: 10 minutes | Cook time: 32 minutes**

### Cinnamon-Apple Crisps | Serves 4

- Oil, for spraying
- 2 Red Delicious or Honeycrisp apples
- ¼ teaspoon cinnamon powder, divided

### Kale Crisps with Tex-Mex Dip | Serves 8

- 240 ml Greek yoghurt
- 1 tablespoon chilli powder
- 80 ml low-salt salsa, well drained
- 1 bunch curly kale
- 1 teaspoon olive oil
- ¼ teaspoon coarse sea salt

**For Cinnamon-Apple Crisps:**

1. Line the air fryer basket in Zone 1 with baking paper and lightly spray it with oil.
2. Trim the uneven ends off the apples. Using a mandoline on the thinnest setting or a sharp knife, slice the apples into very thin rounds. Discard the cores.
3. Place the apple slices in a single layer in the prepared basket. Sprinkle them with half of the cinnamon.
4. Place a metal fryer trivet on top of the apples to prevent them from moving around during cooking.
5. Preheat the Ninja Double Stack Air Fryer to 150ºC by selecting the temperature and pressing START/PAUSE to begin. Once preheated, air fry at 150ºC for 16 minutes, flipping the apple slices every 5 minutes to ensure even cooking.
6. Allow the apple crisps to cool to room temperature. They will firm up as they cool and become crispier.

**For Kale Crisps with Tex-Mex Dip:**

1. In a small bowl, combine the yogurt, chili powder, and drained salsa. Mix well, then refrigerate the dip until ready to serve.
2. Rinse the kale thoroughly and pat it dry with paper towels. Remove the stems and ribs from the kale using a sharp knife. Tear or cut the leaves into 3-inch pieces.
3. In a large bowl, toss the kale with olive oil, ensuring each piece is evenly coated.
4. Preheat the Ninja Double Stack Air Fryer to 200ºC by selecting the temperature and pressing START/PAUSE to begin. Once preheated, place the kale in Zone 2 of the air fryer basket in small batches to avoid overcrowding. Air fry for 5 to 6 minutes, or until the leaves are crisp. Shake the basket halfway through for even cooking.
5. As you remove the kale chips, sprinkle them lightly with sea salt for added flavor.
6. Once all of the kale chips are done, serve them immediately with the prepared dip.

# Stuffed Fried Mushrooms

**Prep time: 20 minutes | Cook time: 10 to 11 minutes | Serves 10**

- 50 g panko breadcrumbs
- ½ teaspoon freshly ground black pepper
- ½ teaspoon onion powder
- ½ teaspoon cayenne pepper
- 1 (227 g) package soft white cheese, at room temperature
- 20 cremini or button mushrooms, stemmed
- 1 to 2 tablespoons oil

1. In a medium-sized bowl, whisk the breadcrumbs, black pepper, onion powder, and cayenne until well blended.
2. Add the soft white cheese to the mixture and stir until fully incorporated. Fill each mushroom cap with 1 teaspoon of the cheese mixture.
3. Preheat the Ninja Double Stack Air Fryer to 180ºC by selecting the temperature and pressing START/PAUSE to begin. Line Zone 1 and Zone 2 baskets with a piece of baking paper to prevent sticking.
4. Place the stuffed mushrooms in a single layer in Zone 1 and Zone 2 of the air fryer basket, ensuring there is enough space for air circulation. Lightly spritz the mushrooms with oil.
5. Air fry for 5 minutes. Shake both baskets gently, then continue cooking for an additional 5 to 6 minutes, or until the filling is firm and the mushrooms are tender.

# Herbed Green Lentil Rice Balls

**Prep time: 5 minutes | Cook time: 11 minutes | Serves 6**

- 120 ml cooked green lentils
- 2 garlic cloves, minced
- ¼ white onion, minced
- 60 ml parsley leaves
- 5 basil leaves
- 235 ml cooked brown rice
- 1 tablespoon lemon juice
- 1 tablespoon olive oil
- ½ teaspoon salt

1. Preheat the Ninja Double Stack Air Fryer to 192ºC by selecting the temperature and pressing START/PAUSE to begin.
2. In a food processor, pulse the cooked lentils with garlic, onion, parsley, and basil until mostly smooth. You'll want some lentil bits left in the mixture for texture. Pour the lentil mixture into a large bowl and stir in brown rice, lemon juice, olive oil, and salt. Mix well until everything is fully combined.
3. Form the mixture into 1-inch balls.
4. Arrange the rice balls in a single layer in Zone 1 and Zone 2 of the air fryer basket, making sure they don't touch each other for even cooking.
5. Air fry at 192ºC for 6 minutes.
6. After 6 minutes, turn the rice balls and continue frying for an additional 4 to 5 minutes, or until they are browned on all sides.

## Roasted Mushrooms with Garlic

**Prep time: 3 minutes | Cook time: 22 to 27 minutes | Serves 4**

- 16 garlic cloves, peeled
- 2 teaspoons olive oil, divided
- 16 button mushrooms
- ½ teaspoon dried marjoram
- ⅛ teaspoon freshly ground black pepper
- 1 tablespoon white wine or low-salt mixed vegetables broth

1. In a small bowl, whisk together the soft white cheese, 40g of panko, parsley, and chili powder until fully combined. Stuff the cheese mixture into the halved jalapeños.
2. Sprinkle the tops of the stuffed jalapeños with the remaining 40g of panko and gently press it into the filling.
3. Preheat the Ninja Double Stack Air Fryer by selecting the AIR FRY function, setting the temperature to 190°C, and the time to 3 minutes. Press START/PAUSE to begin.
4. Once the unit is preheated, spray the crisper plate with cooking oil. Place the stuffed jalapeño poppers in Zone 1 and Zone 2 of the air fryer basket, ensuring they are in a single layer.
5. Set the air fryer to AIR FRY at 190°C for 8 minutes. Press START/PAUSE to begin cooking.
6. After 6 minutes, check the poppers. If they are softened and the cheese is melted, they are ready. If not, continue cooking for additional time.
7. Once cooked, remove the poppers from the air fryer and serve warm.

## Fried Artichoke Hearts

**Prep time: 10 minutes | Cook time: 12 minutes | Serves 10**

- Oil, for spraying
- 3 (397 g) tins quartered artichokes, drained and patted dry
- 120 ml mayonnaise
- 180 g panko breadcrumbs
- 50 g grated Parmesan cheese
- Salt and freshly ground black pepper, to taste

1. Line the air fryer basket with baking paper and spray lightly with oil.
2. Place the artichokes on a plate. Put the mayonnaise and breadcrumbs in separate bowls.
3. Working one at a time, dredge each artichoke heart in the mayonnaise, then in the breadcrumbs to coat evenly.
4. Place the artichokes in the prepared basket. Depending on the size of your air fryer, you may need to cook in batches.
5. Select AIR FRY for Zone 1 and Zone 2 of the Ninja Double Stack Air Fryer, set the temperature to 190°C, and set the timer for 10 to 12 minutes. Press MATCH to synchronize both zones and START/STOP to begin cooking. Cook until the artichokes are crispy and golden.
6. Once cooked, sprinkle with Parmesan cheese and season with salt and black pepper. Serve immediately.

## Spicy Lentil Patties

**Prep time: 15 minutes | Cook time: 10 minutes | Serves 4**

- 235 ml cooked brown lentils
- 60 ml fresh parsley leaves
- 120 ml shredded carrots
- ¼ red onion, minced
- ¼ red pepper, minced
- 1 jalapeño, seeded and minced
- 2 garlic cloves, minced
- 1 egg
- 2 tablespoons lemon juice
- 2 tablespoons olive oil, divided
- ½ teaspoon onion powder
- ½ teaspoon smoked paprika
- ½ teaspoon dried oregano
- ¼ teaspoon salt
- ¼ teaspoon black pepper
- 120 ml wholemeal breadcrumbs

For serving:
- Wholemeal buns or wholemeal pittas
- Plain Greek yoghurt
- Tomato
- Lettuce
- Red Onion

1. Preheat the Ninja Double Stack Air Fryer to 192°C by selecting the temperature and pressing START/PAUSE to begin.
2. In a food processor, pulse the lentils and parsley until mostly smooth. (Some bits of lentils should remain in the mixture for texture.) Transfer the lentil mixture to a large bowl and combine with the carrots, onion, pepper, jalapeño, garlic, egg, lemon juice, and 1 tablespoon of olive oil.
3. Add the onion powder, paprika, oregano, salt, pepper, and breadcrumbs to the mixture.
4. Stir everything together until the seasonings and breadcrumbs are well distributed and the mixture is uniform.
5. Form the mixture into 4 patties.
6. Place the patties in Zone 1 and Zone 2 of the air fryer basket in a single layer, making sure the patties don't touch each other for proper air circulation.
7. Brush the remaining 1 tablespoon of olive oil over the patties.
8. Air fry at 192°C for 5 minutes, then flip the patties and air fry for an additional 5 minutes.
9. Serve the patties on toasted wholemeal buns or wholemeal pittas with a spoonful of yogurt and your choice of lettuce, tomato, and red onion.

# Lemony Pear Chips & Mixed Vegetables Pot Stickers

**Prep time: 15 minutes | Cook time: 11 to 18 minutes**

### Lemony Pear Chips | Serves 4

- 2 firm Bosc or Anjou pears, cut crosswise into ⅛-inch-thick slices
- 1 tablespoon freshly squeezed lemon juice
- ½ teaspoon cinnamon powder
- ⅛ teaspoon ground cardamom

### Mixed Vegetables Pot Stickers | Makes 12 pot stickers

- 70 g shredded red cabbage
- 25 g chopped button mushrooms
- 35 g grated carrot
- 2 tablespoons minced onion
- 2 garlic cloves, minced
- 2 teaspoons grated fresh ginger
- 12 gyoza/pot sticker wrappers
- 2½ teaspoons olive oil, divided

### For Lemony Pear Chips:

1. Preheat the Ninja Double Stack Air Fryer to 190°C by selecting the temperature and pressing START/PAUSE to begin.
2. Separate the smaller stem-end pear rounds from the larger rounds with seeds. Remove the core and seeds from the larger slices. Sprinkle all slices with lemon juice, cinnamon, and cardamom.
3. Place the smaller pear slices in Zone 1 of the air fryer basket. Air fry at 190°C for 3 to 5 minutes, or until they are light golden, shaking the basket once halfway through cooking. Once done, remove from the air fryer.
4. Repeat the process with the larger pear slices, placing them in Zone 1 of the air fryer basket. Air fry at 190°C for 6 to 8 minutes, or until golden and crispy, shaking the basket halfway through.
5. Once all the pear crisps are done, remove them from the air fryer. Allow them to cool before serving. Alternatively, store them in an airtight container at room temperature for up to 2 days.

### For Mixed Vegetables Pot Stickers:

1. In a baking pan, combine the red cabbage, mushrooms, carrot, onion, garlic, and ginger. Add 1 tablespoon of water. Preheat the Ninja Double Stack Air Fryer to 190°C by selecting the temperature and pressing START/PAUSE to begin. Once preheated, place the pan in Zone 2 and air fry for 3 to 6 minutes, until the mixed vegetables are crisp-tender. Drain and set aside.
2. Working one at a time, place the pot sticker wrappers on a clean work surface. Top each wrapper with a scant 1 tablespoon of the vegetable filling. Fold half of the wrapper over the other half to form a half circle. Dab one edge with water and press both edges together to seal.
3. Add 1¼ teaspoons of olive oil to a second pan. Place half of the pot stickers, seam-side up, into the pan. Arrange the pan in Zone 2 of the air fryer basket. Air fry for 5 minutes, or until the bottoms are light golden.
4. Add 1 tablespoon of water to the pan, then return it to the air fryer. Air fry for an additional 4 to 6 minutes, or until the pot stickers are hot throughout.
5. Repeat the process with the remaining pot stickers, 1¼ teaspoons of olive oil, and another tablespoon of water in Zone 2.
6. Once cooked, serve the pot stickers immediately.

# Hush Puppies

**Prep time: 45 minutes | Cook time: 10 minutes | Serves 12**

- 144 g self-raising yellow cornmeal
- 60 g plain flour
- 1 teaspoon sugar
- 1 teaspoon salt
- 1 teaspoon freshly ground black pepper
- 1 large egg
- 80 g canned creamed sweetcorn
- 216 g minced onion
- 2 teaspoons minced jalapeño chillies pepper
- 2 tablespoons olive oil, divided

1. Thoroughly combine the cornmeal, flour, sugar, salt, and pepper in a large bowl. 2. Whisk together the egg and sweetcorn in a small bowl. Pour the egg mixture into the bowl of cornmeal mixture and stir to combine. Stir in the minced onion and jalapeño chillies. Cover the bowl with cling film and place in the refrigerator for 30 minutes. 3. Preheat the air fryer to 190°C. Line the air fryer basket with baking paper paper and lightly brush it with 1 tablespoon of olive oil. 4. Scoop out the cornmeal mixture and form into 24 balls, about 1 inch. 5. Arrange the balls in the baking paper paper-lined basket, leaving space between each ball. 6. Air fry in batches for 5 minutes. Shake the basket and brush the balls with the remaining 1 tablespoon of olive oil. Continue cooking for 5 minutes until golden. 7. Remove the balls (hush puppies) from the basket and serve on a plate.

# Italian Rice Balls & Fried Dill Pickles with Buttermilk Dressing

**Prep time: 45 minutes | Cook time: 10 minutes | Makes 8 rice balls**

- 355 g cooked sticky rice
- ½ teaspoon Italian seasoning blend
- ¾ teaspoon salt, divided
- 8 black olives, pitted
- 28 g mozzarella cheese, cut into tiny pieces (small enough to stuff into olives)
- 2 eggs
- 35 g Italian breadcrumbs
- 55 g panko breadcrumbs
- Cooking spray

**Fried Dill Pickles with Buttermilk Dressing | Serves 6 to 8**

Buttermilk Dressing:
- 60 ml buttermilk
- 60 g chopped spring onions
- 180 ml mayonnaise
- 120 ml sour cream
- ½ teaspoon cayenne pepper

Fried Dill Pickles:
- 90 g plain flour
- 1 (900 g) jar kosher dill pickles, cut into 4 spears, drained
- 300 g panko breadcrumbs
- ½ teaspoon onion powder
- ½ teaspoon garlic powder
- 1 tablespoon chopped chives
- 2 tablespoons chopped fresh dill
- Rock salt and ground black pepper, to taste
- 2 eggs, beaten with 2 tablespoons water
- Rock salt and ground black pepper, to taste
- Cooking spray

**For Italian Rice Balls:**

1. Preheat the Ninja Double Stack Air Fryer to 200°C by selecting the temperature and pressing START/PAUSE to begin.
2. Stuff each black olive with a piece of mozzarella cheese and set aside.
3. In a bowl, combine the cooked sticky rice, Italian seasoning blend, and ½ teaspoon of salt. Stir to mix well. Form the rice mixture into a log, divide it into 8 equal portions, and mold each portion around a stuffed black olive to form a ball.
4. Transfer the rice balls to the freezer to chill for 10 to 15 minutes, or until firm.
5. In a shallow dish, place the Italian breadcrumbs. In a second shallow dish, whisk the eggs. In a third shallow dish, combine the panko breadcrumbs and remaining salt.
6. One by one, roll each rice ball in the Italian breadcrumbs, dip it in the whisked eggs, and finally coat it in the panko breadcrumbs.
7. Preheat Zone 1 of the air fryer baskets by selecting the desired temperature and pressing START/PAUSE to begin. Once preheated, arrange the rice balls in Zone 1 in a single layer and spritz both sides with cooking spray.
8. Air fry at 200°C for 10 minutes, flipping the rice balls halfway through the cooking time, until they are golden and crispy.
9. Once cooked, remove the rice balls from the air fryer and serve warm.

**For Fried Dill Pickles with Buttermilk Dressing:**

1. Preheat the Ninja Double Stack Air Fryer to 200°C by selecting the temperature and pressing START/PAUSE to begin.
2. In a bowl, combine the ingredients for the dressing. Stir well to mix everything together.
3. Cover the bowl with plastic wrap and refrigerate for 30 minutes, or until ready to serve.
4. Pour the flour into a bowl and sprinkle with salt and ground black pepper. Stir to combine the seasonings evenly.
5. Place the breadcrumbs in a separate bowl.
6. In a third bowl, pour the beaten eggs.
7. Dredge each pickle spear in the flour mixture, then dip it into the beaten eggs, and finally coat it with the breadcrumbs, making sure each spear is evenly coated. Shake off any excess coating.
8. Arrange the coated pickle spears in Zone 2 of the air fryer basket, ensuring they are placed in a single layer with space between them for even cooking. Spritz the spears lightly with cooking spray.
9. Air fry at 200°C for 8 minutes, flipping the pickle spears halfway through the cooking time to ensure they crisp up evenly on both sides.
10. Once cooked, serve the crispy pickle spears with the chilled buttermilk dressing.

# Chapter 8
## Vegetables and Sides

# Chapter 8 Vegetables and Sides

## Chiles Rellenos with Red Chile Sauce & Banger-Stuffed Mushroom Caps

**Prep time: 20 minutes | Cook time: 20 minutes**

### Chiles Rellenos with Red Chile Sauce | Serves 2

Peppers:
- 2 poblano peppers, rinsed and dried
- 110 g thawed frozen or drained canned maize kernels
- 1 spring onion, sliced

Sauce:
- 3 tablespoons extra-virgin olive oil
- 25 g finely chopped brown onion
- 2 teaspoons minced garlic
- 1 (170 g) tin tomato paste
- 2 tablespoons ancho chilli powder
- 1 teaspoon dried
- 2 tablespoons chopped fresh coriander
- ½ teaspoon coarse sea salt
- ¼ teaspoon black pepper
- 150 g grated Monterey Jack cheese
- oregano
- 1 teaspoon ground cumin
- ½ teaspoon coarse sea salt
- 470 ml chicken stock
- 2 tablespoons fresh lemon juice
- Mexican crema or sour cream, for serving

### Banger-Stuffed Mushroom Caps | Serves 2

- 6 large portobello mushroom caps
- 230 g Italian banger
- 15 g chopped onion
- 2 tablespoons blanched finely ground almond flour
- 20 g grated Parmesan cheese
- 1 teaspoon minced fresh garlic

**For Chiles Rellenos with Red Chile Sauce:**

**For the Peppers:**

1. Place the peppers in Zone 1 or Zone 2 of the air fryer basket. Set the air fryer to 200°C for 10 minutes, turning the peppers halfway through the cooking time. Air fry until the skins are charred. Once done, transfer the peppers to a resealable plastic bag, seal it, and set aside to steam for 5 minutes.
2. After 5 minutes, peel the skins off the peppers and discard them. Cut a slit down the center of each pepper, starting at the stem and continuing to the tip. Remove the seeds carefully, being sure not to tear the peppers.

**For the Filling:**

3. In a medium bowl, combine the maize, spring onion, coriander, salt, black pepper, and cheese. Set the mixture aside.

For the Sauce:

4. In a large frying pan, heat the olive oil over medium-high heat. Add the onion and cook, stirring occasionally, until tender, about 5 minutes. Add the garlic and cook for 30 seconds more.
5. Stir in the tomato paste, chili powder, oregano, cumin, and salt. Cook, stirring, for 1 minute. Then whisk in the stock and lemon juice. Bring to a simmer and cook, stirring occasionally, while the stuffed peppers finish cooking.

Stuffing the Peppers:

6. Carefully stuff each pepper with half of the maize mixture. Place the stuffed peppers in a baking pan.
7. Preheat the Ninja Double Stack Air Fryer to 200°C by selecting the temperature and pressing START/PAUSE to begin. Once preheated, place the pan with the stuffed peppers in Zone 1 of the air fryer basket. Air fry at 200°C for 10 minutes, or until the cheese has melted.
8. Transfer the stuffed peppers to a serving platter. Drizzle with the sauce and top with some crema

**For Banger-Stuffed Mushroom Caps:**

1. Use a spoon to hollow out each mushroom cap, reserving the scrapings for later use.
2. In a medium frying pan over medium heat, brown the banger for about 10 minutes, or until fully cooked and no pink remains. Drain any excess fat, then add the reserved mushroom scrapings, onion, almond flour, Parmesan cheese, and garlic to the pan. Gently fold the ingredients together and continue cooking for an additional minute, then remove from heat.
3. Evenly spoon the mixture into the hollowed-out mushroom caps. Place the filled caps into a 6-inch round pan that will fit in the air fryer.
4. Preheat the Ninja Double Stack Air Fryer to 190°C by selecting the temperature and pressing START/PAUSE to begin. Once preheated, place the pan with the stuffed mushrooms in Zone 2 of the air fryer basket.
5. Air fry at 190°C for 8 minutes. Once finished, the tops of the mushrooms will be browned and bubbling.
6. Remove from the air fryer and serve warm.

# Roasted Radishes with Sea Salt & Broccoli-Cheddar Twice-Baked Potatoes

**Prep time: 5 minutes | Cook time: 18 minutes**

### Roasted Radishes with Sea Salt | Serves 4

- 450 g radishes, ends trimmed if needed
- 2 tablespoons olive oil
- ½ teaspoon sea salt

### Broccoli-Cheddar Twice-Baked Potatoes | Serves 4

- Oil, for spraying
- 2 medium Maris Piper potatoes
- 1 tablespoon olive oil
- 30 g broccoli florets
- 1 tablespoon sour cream
- 1 teaspoon garlic powder
- 1 teaspoon onion powder
- 60 g shredded Cheddar cheese

For Roasted Radishes with Sea Salt:

1. Preheat the Ninja Double Stack Air Fryer to 180°C by selecting the temperature and pressing START/PAUSE to begin.
2. In a large bowl, combine the radishes with olive oil and sea salt, tossing them to coat evenly.
3. Place the radishes in a single layer in Zone 1 of the air fryer basket, ensuring they are spread out for even cooking.
4. Air fry at 180°C for 10 minutes. After 10 minutes, stir or turn the radishes over for even roasting. Continue air frying for an additional 8 minutes, or until the radishes are tender and lightly browned.
5. Once cooked, remove the radishes from the air fryer and serve immediately.

For Broccoli-Cheddar Twice-Baked Potatoes:

1. Line the air fryer basket in Zone 2 with parchment paper and lightly spray with oil.
2. Rinse the potatoes thoroughly and pat dry with paper towels. Rub the outside of each potato with olive oil, then place them in the prepared basket.
3. Preheat the Ninja Double Stack Air Fryer to 200°C by selecting the temperature and pressing START/PAUSE to begin. Once preheated, air fry the potatoes at 200°C for 40 minutes, or until they are easily pierced with a fork. Let the potatoes cool just enough to handle, then cut them in half lengthwise.
4. Meanwhile, place the broccoli in a microwave-safe bowl, cover with water, and microwave on high for 5 to 8 minutes. Drain the broccoli and set aside.
5. Scoop out most of the potato flesh from each half and transfer to a medium-sized bowl.
6. Add the sour cream, garlic, and onion powder to the bowl, stirring until the potatoes are mashed and well combined.
7. Spoon the mashed potato mixture back into the hollowed-out potato skins, mounding the mixture as necessary. Top with the steamed broccoli and cheese. Return the stuffed potatoes to the basket in Zone 2. Depending on the size of your air fryer, you may need to work in batches.
8. Air fry at 200°C for 3 to 6 minutes, or until the cheese has melted and is bubbly.
9. Once done, remove the stuffed potatoes from the air fryer and serve immediately.

# Buffalo Cauliflower with Blue Cheese

**Prep time: 15 minutes | Cook time: 5 to 7 minutes per batch | Serves 6**

- 1 large head cauliflower, rinsed and separated into small florets
- 1 tablespoon extra-virgin olive oil
- ½ teaspoon garlic powder
- Cooking oil spray
- 80 ml hot wing sauce
- 190 g nonfat Greek yoghurt
- 60 g buttermilk
- ½ teaspoon hot sauce
- 1 celery stick, chopped
- 2 tablespoons crumbled blue cheese

1. Insert the crisper plate into Zone 1 and Zone 2 of the air fryer basket. Preheat the Ninja Double Stack Air Fryer by selecting the AIR FRY function, setting the temperature to 190°C, and the time to 3 minutes. Press START/PAUSE to begin preheating.
2. In a large bowl, toss the cauliflower florets with olive oil. Sprinkle with garlic powder and toss again to coat evenly.
3. Once preheated, spray the crisper plate with cooking oil. Add half of the cauliflower to Zone 1 and Zone 2 of the air fryer basket in a single layer.
4. Select AIR FRY, set the temperature to 190°C, and set the time to 7 minutes. Press START/PAUSE to begin cooking.
5. After 3 minutes, remove the basket and shake the cauliflower for even cooking. Reinsert the basket to resume cooking. After 2 minutes, check the cauliflower. It is done when it is browned and crispy. If not, continue cooking for additional time.
6. Once cooked, transfer the cauliflower to a serving bowl and toss with half of the hot wing sauce.
7. Repeat steps 4, 5, and 6 with the remaining cauliflower and hot wing sauce.
8. In a small bowl, stir together the yogurt, buttermilk, hot sauce, celery, and blue cheese. Drizzle the sauce over the finished cauliflower and serve immediately.

# Sweet-and-Sour Brussels Sprouts & Cheese-Walnut Stuffed Mushrooms

**Prep time: 10 minutes | Cook time: 20 minutes**

### Sweet-and-Sour Brussels Sprouts | Serves 2

- 70 g Thai sweet chilli sauce
- 2 tablespoons black vinegar or balsamic vinegar
- ½ teaspoon hot sauce, such as Tabasco
- 230 g Brussels sprouts, trimmed (large sprouts halved)
- 2 small shallots, cut into ¼-inch-thick slices
- coarse sea salt and freshly ground black pepper, to taste
- 2 teaspoons lightly packed fresh coriander leaves

### Cheese-Walnut Stuffed Mushrooms | Serves 4

- 4 large portobello mushrooms
- 1 tablespoon rapeseed oil
- 110 g shredded Mozzarella cheese
- 35 g minced walnuts
- 2 tablespoons chopped fresh parsley
- Cooking spray

**For Sweet-and-Sour Brussels Sprouts:**

1. In a large bowl, whisk together the chilli sauce, vinegar, and hot sauce. Add the Brussels sprouts and shallots, season with salt and pepper, and toss to combine. Scrape the Brussels sprouts and sauce into a cake pan.
2. Insert the cake pan into Zone 1 of the Ninja Double Stack Air Fryer. Set Zone 1 to AIR FRY at 190ºC and cook for 20 minutes, stirring every 5 minutes to ensure even roasting and glaze distribution. Press START/PAUSE to begin.
3. Once the Brussels sprouts are tender and the sauce is reduced to a sticky glaze, remove the pan from the air fryer. Transfer the Brussels sprouts to serving plates, sprinkle with coriander, and serve warm.

**For Cheese-Walnut Stuffed Mushrooms:**

1. Preheat the Ninja Double Stack Air Fryer to 180ºC by selecting AIR FRY and setting the timer to 3 minutes. Press START/PAUSE to begin, then lightly spritz the crisper plates in Zone 2 with cooking spray.
2. On a clean work surface, remove the mushroom stems and scoop out the gills using a spoon. Discard the gills and stems, then coat the mushrooms evenly with rapeseed oil. Top each mushroom with shredded Mozzarella cheese, followed by the minced walnuts.
3. Arrange the mushrooms in a single layer in Zone 2 of the air fryer. Set Zone 2 to AIR FRY at 180ºC for 10 minutes. Press MATCH to synchronize the zones and START/PAUSE to begin cooking.
4. Once the mushrooms are golden brown, remove them carefully from the air fryer and transfer them to a serving plate. Sprinkle with parsley for garnish and serve warm.

# Super Cheesy Gold Aubergine

**Prep time: 15 minutes | Cook time: 30 minutes | Serves 4**

- 1 medium aubergine, peeled and cut into ½-inch-thick rounds
- 1 teaspoon salt, plus more for seasoning
- 60 g plain flour
- 2 eggs
- 90 g Italian bread crumbs
- 2 tablespoons grated Parmesan cheese
- Freshly ground black pepper, to taste
- Cooking oil spray
- 180 g marinara sauce
- 45 g shredded Parmesan cheese, divided
- 110 g shredded Mozzarella cheese, divided

1. Blot the aubergine slices thoroughly with paper towels to remove excess moisture. For optimal results, sprinkle the slices with 1 teaspoon of salt to draw out additional moisture, then rinse and blot dry again.
2. Place the flour in a shallow bowl. In a second bowl, beat the eggs until smooth. In a third bowl, mix the bread crumbs with grated Parmesan cheese, seasoning with salt and pepper to taste.
3. Coat each aubergine slice by dipping it first into the flour, then into the beaten eggs, and finally into the bread crumb mixture, ensuring an even coating on all sides.
4. Insert crisper plates into Zone 1 and Zone 2 of the Ninja Double Stack Air Fryer baskets. Preheat both zones by selecting AIR FRY, setting the temperature to 200ºC, and setting the time to 3 minutes. Press START/PAUSE to begin.
5. Once preheated, spray the crisper plates and baskets with cooking oil. Arrange the coated aubergine slices in a single layer across both baskets, ensuring no overlap for even cooking. Lightly spray the tops of the aubergine slices with oil.
6. Set both zones to AIR FRY at 200ºC and adjust the time to 10 minutes. Press MATCH to synchronize the zones and START/PAUSE to begin cooking.
7. After 7 minutes of cooking, open the baskets and top each aubergine slice with 1 teaspoon of marinara sauce, ½ tablespoon of shredded Parmesan, and ½ tablespoon of Mozzarella cheese. Close the baskets and resume cooking for an additional 2 to 3 minutes until the cheese is melted and bubbly.
8. Repeat steps 3 through 7 for any remaining aubergine slices to ensure all are evenly cooked and topped.
9. When all batches are complete, remove the cooked aubergine slices from the baskets and serve immediately while warm for the best flavor.

## Maize Croquettes & Garlicky Baked Cherry Tomatoes

**Prep time: 10 minutes | Cook time: 12 to 14 minutes**

### Maize Croquettes | Serves 4

- 105 g leftover mashed potatoes
- 340 g maize kernels (if frozen, thawed, and well drained)
- ¼ teaspoon onion powder
- ⅛ teaspoon ground black pepper
- ¼ teaspoon salt
- 50 g panko bread crumbs
- Oil for misting or cooking spray

### Dijon Roast Cabbage | Serves 4

- Garlicky Baked Cherry Tomatoes | Serves 2
- 475 g cherry tomatoes
- 1 clove garlic, thinly sliced
- 1 teaspoon olive oil
- ⅛ teaspoon rock salt
- 1 tablespoon freshly chopped basil, for topping
- Cooking spray

**For Garlicky Baked Cherry Tomatoes:**

1. Add the potatoes and half of the maize to a food processor, pulsing until the maize is finely chopped and blended evenly with the potatoes.
2. Transfer the mixture into a large bowl and add the remaining maize, onion powder, pepper, and salt. Stir the mixture thoroughly until fully combined.
3. Divide the mixture into 16 equal portions and shape each into a ball, ensuring they are consistent in size and compact for even cooking.
3. Roll each ball in panko crumbs until evenly coated, then lightly mist with oil or cooking spray. Place the balls evenly in Zone 1..
1. Select the AIR FRY function, set the temperature to 180ºC, and the timer to 12 minutes. Press the MATCH button to synchronize cooking and START/PAUSE to begin. Check after 12 minutes to ensure they are golden brown and crispy, adding 1 to 2 more minutes if needed. Remove and serve hot.

**For Garlicky Baked Cherry Tomatoes:**

1. Preheat the Ninja Double Stack Air Fryer to 180ºC by selecting AIR FRY and setting the timer to 3 minutes. Press START/PAUSE to begin, then lightly spritz the crisper plates in Zone 2 with cooking spray.
2. On a clean work surface, remove the mushroom stems and scoop out the gills using a spoon. Discard the gills and stems, then coat the mushrooms evenly with rapeseed oil. Top each mushroom with shredded Mozzarella cheese, followed by the minced walnuts.
3. Arrange the mushrooms in a single layer. Set AIR FRY at 180ºC for 10 minutes. Press MATCH to synchronize the zones and START/PAUSE to begin cooking.
4. Once the mushrooms are golden brown, remove them carefully from the air fryer and transfer them to a serving plate. Sprinkle with parsley for garnish and serve warm.

## Fig, Chickpea, and Rocket Salad

**Prep time: 15 minutes | Cook time: 20 minutes | Serves 4**

- 8 fresh figs, halved
- 250 g cooked chickpeas
- 1 teaspoon crushed roasted cumin seeds
- 4 tablespoons balsamic vinegar
- 2 tablespoons extra-virgin olive oil, plus more for greasing
- Salt and ground black pepper, to taste
- 40 g rocket, washed and dried

1. Preheat the Ninja Double Stack Air Fryer to 190ºC by selecting the temperature and pressing START/PAUSE to begin.
2. Cover the air fryer basket in Zone 1 and Zone 2 with aluminium foil and lightly grease with oil. Place the figs in Zone 1 and Zone 2 of the air fryer basket. Air fry for 10 minutes.
3. In a bowl, combine the chickpeas and cumin seeds.
4. Once the figs are done, remove them from the air fryer and replace with the chickpeas. Air fry at 190ºC for 10 minutes. Once done, leave the chickpeas to cool.
5. While the chickpeas are cooling, prepare the dressing by mixing balsamic vinegar, olive oil, salt, and pepper in a small bowl.
6. In a salad bowl, combine the rocket with the cooled figs and chickpeas.
7. Toss with the dressing and serve immediately.

# Chermoula-Roasted Beetroots & Blistered Shishito Peppers with Lime Juice

**Prep time: 15 minutes | Cook time: 25 minutes**

### Chermoula-Roasted Beetroots | Serves 4

Chermoula:

- 30 g packed fresh coriander leaves
- 15 g packed fresh parsley leaves
- 6 cloves garlic, peeled
- 2 teaspoons smoked paprika
- 2 teaspoons ground cumin
- 1 teaspoon ground coriander
- ½ to 1 teaspoon cayenne pepper
- Pinch crushed saffron (optional)
- 115 g extra-virgin olive oil
- coarse sea salt, to taste

Beetroots:

- 3 medium beetroots, trimmed, peeled, and cut into 1-inch chunks
- 2 tablespoons chopped fresh coriander
- 2 tablespoons chopped fresh parsley

### Blistered Shishito Peppers with Lime Juice | Serves 3

- 230 g shishito peppers, rinsed
- Cooking spray

Sauce:

- 1 tablespoon tamari or shoyu
- 2 teaspoons fresh lime juice
- 2 large garlic cloves, minced

### For Chermoula-Roasted Beetroots :

1. For the chermoula: In a food processor, combine the fresh coriander, parsley, garlic, paprika, cumin, ground coriander, and cayenne. Pulse until coarsely chopped. Add the saffron (if using) and process until combined. With the food processor running, slowly add the olive oil in a steady stream and process until the sauce is uniform. Season to taste with salt.
2. For the beetroots: In a large bowl, drizzle the beetroots with ½ cup of the chermoula, or enough to coat them evenly. Arrange the beetroots in Zone 2 of the Ninja Double Stack Air Fryer basket.
3. Select AIR FRY for both zones, set the temperature to 190ºC, and the timer to 25 minutes. Press MATCH to synchronize both zones and START/STOP to begin cooking. Cook until the beetroots are tender.
4. Transfer the beetroots to a serving platter. Sprinkle with chopped coriander and parsley and serve immediately.

### For Blistered Shishito Peppers with Lime Juice:

1. Preheat Zone 2 of the Ninja Double Stack Air Fryer to 200ºC by selecting AIR FRY and pressing MATCH, then START/STOP.
2. Place the shishito peppers in Zone 2 of the air fryer basket, and spritz them lightly with cooking spray.
3. Select AIR FRY and cook for 3 minutes.
4. Meanwhile, whisk together all the ingredients for the sauce in a large bowl. Set aside.
5. Shake the basket gently and spritz the peppers with cooking spray again. Cook for an additional 3 minutes in both zones.
6. Shake the basket again, spray the peppers with cooking spray, and continue roasting for another 3 minutes until the peppers are blistered and browned.
7. Once done, remove the peppers from Zone 2 and transfer them to the bowl of sauce. Toss well to coat and serve immediately.

# Parmesan-Rosemary Radishes

**Prep time: 5 minutes | Cook time: 15 to 20 minutes | Serves 4**

- 1 bunch radishes, stemmed, trimmed, and quartered
- 1 tablespoon avocado oil
- 2 tablespoons finely grated fresh Parmesan cheese
- 1 tablespoon chopped fresh rosemary
- Sea salt and freshly ground black pepper, to taste

1. Place the radishes in a medium bowl and toss them with avocado oil, Parmesan cheese, rosemary, salt, and pepper until evenly coated.
2. Preheat both Zone 1 and Zone 2 of the Ninja Double Stack Air Fryer to 190ºC by selecting AIR FRY and pressing MATCH, then START/STOP.
3. Arrange the radishes in a single layer in Zone 1 and Zone 2 of the air fryer basket.
4. Select AIR FRY for both zones and set the timer for 15 to 20 minutes. Press MATCH to synchronize both zones and START/STOP to begin cooking. Roast until the radishes are golden brown and tender.
5. Once done, remove the radishes from both zones and let cool for 5 minutes before serving.

# Southwestern Roasted Maize

**Prep time: 10 minutes | Cook time: 10 minutes | Serves 4**

maize:
- 240 g thawed frozen maize kernels
- 50 g diced brown onion
- 150 g mixed diced peppers
- 1 jalapeño, diced
- 1 tablespoon fresh lemon juice
- 1 teaspoon ground cumin
- ½ teaspoon ancho chilli powder
- ½ teaspoon coarse sea salt

For Serving:
- 150 g queso fresco or feta cheese
- 10 g chopped fresh coriander
- 1 tablespoon fresh lemon juice

1. For the maize: In a large bowl, stir together the maize, onion, peppers, jalapeño, lemon juice, cumin, chili powder, and salt until well incorporated.
2. Preheat the Ninja Double Stack Air Fryer to 190°C by selecting the temperature and pressing START/PAUSE to begin. Once preheated, pour the spiced vegetables into Zone 1 and Zone 2 of the air fryer basket. Air fry at 190°C for 10 minutes, stirring halfway through the cooking time for even cooking.
3. Once cooked, transfer the maize mixture to a serving bowl. Add the cheese, coriander, and lemon juice, and stir well to combine. Serve immediately.

# Polenta Casserole

**Prep time: 5 minutes | Cook time: 28 to 30 minutes | Serves 4**

- 10 fresh asparagus spears, cut into 1-inch pieces
- 320 g cooked polenta, cooled to room temperature
- 1 egg, beaten
- 2 teaspoons Worcestershire sauce
- ½ teaspoon garlic powder
- ¼ teaspoon salt
- 2 slices emmental cheese (about 40 g)
- Oil for misting or cooking spray

1. Mist the asparagus spears with oil and place them in Zone 1 and Zone 2 of the air fryer basket. Air fry at 200°C for 5 minutes, until crisp-tender.
2. In a medium bowl, mix together the coarse cornmeal, egg, Worcestershire sauce, garlic powder, and salt.
3. Spoon half of the polenta mixture into a baking pan that fits in the air fryer basket. Top with the air fried asparagus.
4. Tear the cheese slices into pieces and layer them evenly on top of the asparagus.
5. Top with the remaining polenta mixture, spreading it evenly over the cheese.
6. Place the baking pan into Zone 1 or Zone 2 of the air fryer basket. Set the temperature to 180°C and bake for 23 to 25 minutes. The casserole will rise a little as it cooks. When done, the top will have browned lightly with just a hint of crispiness.

# Courgette Fritters

**Prep time: 10 minutes | Cook time: 10 minutes | Serves 4**

- 2 courgette, grated (about 450 g)
- 1 teaspoon salt
- 25 g almond flour
- 20 g grated Parmesan cheese
- 1 large egg
- ¼ teaspoon dried thyme
- ¼ teaspoon ground turmeric
- ¼ teaspoon freshly ground black pepper
- 1 tablespoon olive oil
- ½ lemon, sliced into wedges

1. Preheat the Ninja Double Stack Air Fryer to 200°C by selecting the temperature and pressing START/PAUSE to begin. Cut a piece of parchment paper to fit slightly smaller than the bottom of the air fryer basket.
2. Place the courgette in a large colander and sprinkle with salt. Let sit for 5 to 10 minutes. Squeeze out as much liquid as possible from the courgette and transfer it to a large mixing bowl. Add the almond flour, Parmesan, egg, thyme, turmeric, and black pepper. Stir gently until thoroughly combined.
3. Shape the mixture into 8 patties and arrange them on the parchment paper. Brush the patties lightly with olive oil.
4. Place the parchment paper with the patties in Zone 1 and Zone 2 of the air fryer basket. Air fry at 200°C for 10 minutes, pausing halfway through to turn the patties for even cooking.
5. Once golden brown and cooked through, remove the patties from the air fryer and serve warm with lemon wedges.

# Garlic Cauliflower with Tahini

**Prep time: 10 minutes | Cook time: 20 minutes | Serves 4**

Cauliflower:
- 500 g cauliflower florets (about 1 large head)
- 6 garlic cloves, smashed and cut into thirds
- 3 tablespoons vegetable oil

Sauce:
- 2 tablespoons tahini (sesame paste)
- 2 tablespoons hot water
- 1 tablespoon fresh lemon juice
- ½ teaspoon ground cumin
- ½ teaspoon ground coriander
- ½ teaspoon coarse sea salt
- 1 teaspoon minced garlic
- ½ teaspoon coarse sea salt

1. For the cauliflower: In a large bowl, combine the cauliflower florets and garlic. Drizzle with vegetable oil and sprinkle with cumin, coriander, and salt. Toss until the florets are evenly coated.
2. Divide the cauliflower evenly between Zone 1 and Zone 2 of the Ninja Double Stack Air Fryer for maximum efficiency. Select AIR FRY for both zones, set the temperature to 200°C, and the timer to 20 minutes. Press MATCH to synchronize the zones and START/PAUSE to begin cooking. Turn the cauliflower halfway through the cooking time for even roasting.
3. Meanwhile, for the sauce: In a small bowl, combine the tahini, water, lemon juice, garlic, and salt. Stir continuously until the mixture transforms into a thick, creamy, and smooth sauce.
4. Once the cauliflower is cooked, transfer it to a large serving bowl. Pour the tahini sauce over the cauliflower and toss gently to coat. Serve immediately while warm.

# Rosemary-Roasted Red Potatoes

**Prep time: 5 minutes | Cook time: 20 minutes | Serves 6**

- 450 g red potatoes, quartered
- 65 ml olive oil
- ½ teaspoon coarse sea salt
- ¼ teaspoon black pepper
- 1 garlic clove, minced
- 4 rosemary sprigs

1. Preheat the air fryer to 180°C. 2. In a large bowl, toss the potatoes with the olive oil, salt, pepper, and garlic until well coated. 3. Pour the potatoes into the air fryer basket and top with the sprigs of rosemary. 4. Roast for 10 minutes, then stir or toss the potatoes and roast for 10 minutes more. 5. Remove the rosemary sprigs and serve the potatoes. Season with additional salt and pepper, if needed.1. Preheat the Ninja Double Stack Air Fryer to 180°C by selecting the temperature and pressing START/PAUSE to begin.
2. In a large bowl, toss the potatoes with the olive oil, salt, pepper, and garlic until they are evenly coated.
3. Transfer the potatoes to Zone 1 and Zone 2 of the air fryer basket, ensuring they are spread out in an even layer. Top the potatoes with the sprigs of rosemary.
4. Air fry at 180°C for 10 minutes, then stir or toss the potatoes and roast for an additional 10 minutes, until they are golden and crispy.
5. Once done, remove the rosemary sprigs and serve the potatoes. Season with additional salt and pepper, if needed.

# Chapter 9
# Vegetarian Mains

# Chapter 9 Vegetarian Mains

## Cauliflower, Chickpea, and Avocado Mash & Italian Baked Egg and Veggies

**Prep time: 10 minutes | Cook time: 25 minutes**

### Cauliflower, Chickpea, and Avocado Mash | Serves 4

- 1 medium head cauliflower, cut into florets
- 1 tin chickpeas, drained and rinsed
- 1 tablespoon extra-virgin olive oil
- 2 tablespoons lemon juice
- Salt and ground black pepper, to taste
- 4 flatbreads, toasted
- 2 ripe avocados, mashed

### Italian Baked Egg and Veggies | Serves 2

- 2 tablespoons salted butter
- 1 small courgette, sliced lengthwise and quartered
- ½ medium green pepper, seeded and diced
- 235 g fresh spinach, chopped
- 1 medium plum tomato, diced
- 2 large eggs
- ¼ teaspoon onion powder
- ¼ teaspoon garlic powder
- ½ teaspoon dried basil
- ¼ teaspoon dried oregano

**For Cauliflower, Chickpea, and Avocado Mash:**

1. Preheat Zone 1 to 220°C by selecting AIR FRY and setting the timer to 3 minutes. Press START/PAUSE to begin.
2. In a bowl, combine the chickpeas, cauliflower, lemon juice, and olive oil. Mix thoroughly to ensure everything is well coated.
3. Season the mixture with salt and pepper to taste, adjusting as needed.
4. Place the seasoned mixture in a single layer in Zone 1 of the air fryer basket. Select AIR FRY at 220°C and set the timer for 25 minutes. Press START/PAUSE to begin cooking. Shake the basket halfway through to ensure even roasting.
5. Once the chickpeas and cauliflower are roasted and golden, spread them evenly on top of the flatbread along with the mashed avocado.
6. Sprinkle with additional salt and pepper if desired, and serve immediately for a delicious and fresh dish.

**For Italian Baked Egg and Veggies:**

1. Grease two ramekins with 1 tablespoon of butter each, ensuring even coverage.
2. In a large bowl, combine the courgette, pepper, spinach, and tomato. Toss until well mixed.
3. Divide the vegetable mixture evenly between the two ramekins, filling them halfway.
4. Crack an egg on top of each ramekin and sprinkle with onion powder, garlic powder, basil, and oregano for added flavor.
5. Place the ramekins into Zone 2 of the Ninja Double Stack Air Fryer.
6. Select AIR FRY for Zone 2, set the temperature to 170°C, and adjust the timer to 10 minutes. Press START/PAUSE to begin baking.
7. Once done, carefully remove the ramekins from Zone 2 and serve immediately while warm for the best taste.

## Spinach-Artichoke Stuffed Mushrooms

**Prep time: 10 minutes | Cook time: 10 to 14 minutes | Serves 4**

- 2 tablespoons olive oil
- 4 large portobello mushrooms, stems removed and gills scraped out
- ½ teaspoon salt
- ¼ teaspoon freshly ground pepper
- 110 g goat cheese, crumbled
- 120 g chopped marinated artichoke hearts
- 235 g frozen spinach, thawed and squeezed dry
- 120 g grated Parmesan cheese
- 2 tablespoons chopped fresh parsley

1. Preheat Zone 1 to 200°C by selecting AIR FRY and pressing START/PAUSE.
2. Rub olive oil over the portobello mushrooms until fully coated.
3. Season both sides with salt and black pepper.
4. Place the mushrooms top-side down on a work surface.
5. Combine goat cheese, artichoke hearts, and spinach in a bowl, mashing with a fork until mixed.
6. Divide the mixture among the mushrooms and sprinkle with Parmesan cheese.
7. Place the mushrooms into Zone 1. Select AIR FRY at 200°C and set the timer to 10 minutes. Press START/PAUSE to cook.
8. Check after 10 minutes; cook 2–4 more minutes if needed, until cheese is golden.
9. Top with parsley and serve immediately.

# Roasted Vegetable Mélange with Herbs & Vegetable Burgers

## Roasted Vegetable Mélange with Herbs | Serves 4

- 1 (230 g) package sliced mushrooms
- 1 yellow butternut marrow, sliced
- 1 red pepper, sliced
- 3 cloves garlic, sliced
- 1 tablespoon olive oil
- ½ teaspoon dried basil
- ½ teaspoon dried thyme
- ½ teaspoon dried tarragon

## Vegetable Burgers | Serves 4

- 227 g cremini or chestnut mushrooms
- 2 large egg yolks
- ½ medium courgette, trimmed and chopped
- 60 g peeled and chopped brown onion
- 1 clove garlic, peeled and finely minced
- ½ teaspoon salt
- ¼ teaspoon ground black pepper

**For Roasted Vegetable Mélange with Herbs:**

1. Preheat Zone 1 to 180°C by selecting AIR FRY and setting the timer to 3 minutes. Press START/PAUSE to begin.
2. In a large bowl, toss the mushrooms, marrow, and pepper with the garlic and olive oil until the vegetables are well coated.
3. Add the basil, thyme, and tarragon to the bowl and toss again to evenly distribute the herbs.
4. Spread the vegetable mixture evenly in the basket of Zone 1, ensuring there is no overcrowding for optimal roasting. Select AIR FRY at 180°C and set the timer for 14 to 18 minutes. Press START/PAUSE to begin cooking, shaking the basket halfway through for even results.
5. Once the vegetables are fork-tender, remove the basket from Zone 1 and let the vegetables cool for 5 minutes before serving. Enjoy warm.

**For Vegetable Burgers:**

1. Place all ingredients into a food processor and pulse about twenty times until finely chopped and well combined.
2. Divide the mixture into four equal portions and shape each into a burger patty.
3. Place the burger patties into Zone 2 of the Ninja Double Stack Air Fryer. Select AIR FRY, set the temperature to 190°C, and the timer to 12 minutes. Press START/PAUSE to begin cooking.
4. Turn the burgers halfway through cooking to ensure even browning on both sides.
5. Check for doneness; the burgers should be browned and firm. Once done, remove from Zone 2 and transfer to a large plate.
6. Allow the burgers to cool for 5 minutes before serving for the best texture and flavor.

# Garlic White Courgette Rolls

**Prep time: 20 minutes | Cook time: 20 minutes | Serves 4**

- 2 medium courgette
- 2 tablespoons unsalted butter
- ¼ white onion, peeled and diced
- ½ teaspoon finely minced roasted garlic
- 60 ml double cream
- 2 tablespoons vegetable broth
- ⅛ teaspoon xanthan gum
- 120 g full-fat ricotta cheese
- ¼ teaspoon salt
- ½ teaspoon garlic powder
- ¼ teaspoon dried oregano
- 475 g spinach, chopped
- 120 g sliced baby portobello mushrooms
- 180 g shredded Mozzarella cheese, divided

1. Using a mandoline or sharp knife, slice the courgette lengthwise into long strips. Place the strips between paper towels to absorb excess moisture and set aside.
2. In a medium saucepan over medium heat, melt the butter. Add the onion and sauté until fragrant, then stir in the garlic and sauté for an additional 30 seconds.
3. Pour in the double cream, broth, and xanthan gum, stirring to combine. Turn off the heat and whisk the mixture until it begins to thicken, about 3 minutes.
4. In a medium bowl, combine the ricotta, salt, garlic powder, and oregano, mixing until smooth. Fold in the spinach, mushrooms, and 120 ml of Mozzarella cheese.
5. Pour half of the prepared sauce into the bottom of each of two round baking pans. To assemble the rolls, place two courgette strips on a flat work surface, slightly overlapping. Spoon 2 tablespoons of the ricotta mixture onto the strips and roll tightly.
6. Divide the courgette rolls evenly between the two baking pans, placing them seam side down on top of the sauce. Pour the remaining sauce evenly over the rolls in both pans and sprinkle with the remaining Mozzarella cheese.
7. Cover both baking pans with foil and place one pan into Zone 1 and the other into Zone 2 of the Ninja Double Stack Air Fryer. Select AIR FRY for both zones, set the temperature to 180°C, and adjust the timer to 20 minutes. Press MATCH to synchronize the cooking process and press START/PAUSE to begin.
8. In the last 5 minutes of cooking, carefully remove the foil from both pans to allow the cheese to brown. Close the baskets and resume cooking until the tops are golden and bubbly.
9. Once done, remove the baking pans from Zone 1 and Zone 2. Serve the courgette rolls immediately for the best flavor and texture.

# Mediterranean Creamed Green Peas & Roasted Veggie Bowl

**Prep time: 10 minutes | Cook time: 25 minutes**

## Mediterranean Creamed Green Peas | Serves 4

- 235 ml cauliflower florets, fresh or frozen
- ½ white onion, roughly chopped
- 2 tablespoons olive oil
- 120 ml unsweetened almond milk
- 700 ml green peas, fresh or frozen
- 3 garlic cloves, minced
- 2 tablespoons fresh thyme leaves, chopped
- 1 teaspoon fresh rosemary leaves, chopped
- ½ teaspoon salt
- ½ teaspoon black pepper
- Shredded Parmesan cheese, for garnish
- Fresh parsley, for garnish

## Roasted Veggie Bowl | Serves 2

**Prep time: 10 minutes | Cook time: 15 minutes**

- 235 g broccoli florets
- 235 g quartered Brussels sprouts
- 120 g cauliflower florets
- ¼ medium white onion, peeled and sliced ¼ inch thick
- ½ medium green pepper, seeded and sliced ¼ inch thick
- 1 tablespoon coconut oil
- 2 teaspoons chilli powder
- ½ teaspoon garlic powder
- ½ teaspoon cumin

### For Mediterranean Creamed Green Peas:

1. Preheat Zone 1 to 192°C by selecting AIR FRY and setting the timer to 3 minutes. Press START/PAUSE to begin.
2. In a large bowl, combine the cauliflower florets and onion with the olive oil. Toss thoroughly to ensure all pieces are evenly coated.
3. Place the cauliflower-and-onion mixture into the basket of Zone 1, spreading it out in an even layer. Select AIR FRY at 192°C and set the timer to 15 minutes. Press START/PAUSE to begin cooking, shaking the basket halfway through for even roasting.
4. Once roasted, transfer the cauliflower and onion to a food processor. Add the almond milk and pulse until the mixture becomes smooth and creamy.
5. In a medium saucepan, combine the cauliflower purée with the peas, garlic, thyme, rosemary, salt, and pepper. Mix well to combine all the ingredients.
6. Cook the mixture over medium heat for 10 minutes, stirring regularly to ensure even cooking and prevent sticking.
7. Serve the finished dish with a sprinkle of Parmesan cheese and freshly chopped parsley for garnish. Enjoy warm.

### For Roasted Veggie Bowl:

1. Toss all the ingredients together in a large bowl, ensuring the vegetables are evenly coated with oil and seasoning.
2. Transfer the vegetables into Zone 2 of the Ninja Double Stack Air Fryer, spreading them out in an even layer to promote even cooking.
3. Select AIR FRY for Zone 2, set the temperature to 180°C, and adjust the timer to 15 minutes. Press START/PAUSE to begin cooking.
4. Shake the basket two or three times during cooking to ensure the vegetables roast evenly.
5. Once done, remove the roasted vegetables from Zone 2 and serve warm for the best flavor.

# Spinach Cheese Casserole & Greek Baked Beans

**Prep time: 15 minutes | Cook time: 30 minutes**

### Spinach Cheese Casserole | Serves 4

- 1 tablespoon salted butter, melted
- 60 g diced brown onion
- 227 g full fat soft white cheese
- 80 g full-fat mayonnaise
- 80 g full-fat sour cream
- 60 g chopped pickled jalapeños
- 475 g fresh spinach, chopped
- 475 g cauliflower florets, chopped
- 235 g artichoke hearts, chopped

### Greek Baked Beans | Serves 4

- Olive oil cooking spray
- 1 (425 g) can cannellini beans, drained and rinsed
- 1 (425 g) can butter beans, drained and rinsed
- ½ brown onion, diced
- 1 (230 g) can tomato sauce
- 1½ tablespoons raw honey
- 60 ml olive oil
- 2 garlic cloves, minced
- 2 tablespoons chopped fresh dill
- ½ teaspoon salt
- ½ teaspoon black pepper
- 1 bay leaf
- 1 tablespoon balsamic vinegar
- 60 g feta cheese, crumbled, for serving

### For Spinach Cheese Casserole:

1. In a large bowl, mix the butter, onion, soft white cheese, mayonnaise, and sour cream until well combined.
2. Fold in the jalapeños, spinach, cauliflower, and artichokes, ensuring an even distribution of ingredients.
3. Transfer the mixture into a round baking dish, smoothing the top for even cooking.
4. Cover the baking dish with foil and place it into Zone 1 of the Ninja Double Stack Air Fryer.
5. Select AIR FRY for Zone 1, set the temperature to 190°C, and adjust the timer to 15 minutes. Press START/PAUSE to begin cooking.
6. In the final 2 minutes of cooking, carefully remove the foil to allow the top to brown. Close the basket and continue cooking until golden and bubbling.
7. Once done, remove the baking dish from Zone 1 and serve the dip warm for the best flavor.

### For Greek Baked Beans:

1. Preheat Zone 2 to 182°C by selecting AIR FRY and setting the timer to 3 minutes. Press START/PAUSE to begin.
2. Lightly coat the inside of a 1.2 L capacity casserole dish with olive oil cooking spray. Ensure the dish fits comfortably in Zone 2 of the air fryer.
3. In a large bowl, combine all ingredients except the feta cheese and stir until the mixture is thoroughly combined.
4. Pour the bean mixture into the prepared casserole dish, spreading it evenly.
5. Place the casserole dish into Zone 2, select AIR FRY, set the temperature to 182°C, and adjust the timer to 30 minutes. Press START/PAUSE to begin baking.
6. Once cooking is complete, carefully remove the casserole dish from Zone 2 and discard the bay leaf.
7. Sprinkle crumbled feta cheese over the top and serve warm for the best flavor.

# Chapter 10
## Desserts

# Chapter 10 Desserts

## Chocolate Chip Pecan Biscotti

**Prep time: 15 minutes | Cook time: 20 to 22 minutes | Serves 10**

- 70 g finely ground blanched almond flour
- ¾ teaspoon baking powder
- ½ teaspoon xanthan gum
- ¼ teaspoon sea salt
- 3 tablespoons unsalted butter, at room temperature
- 35 g powdered sweetener
- 1 large egg, beaten
- 1 teaspoon pure vanilla extract
- 50 g chopped pecans
- 40 g organic chocolate crisps,
- Melted organic chocolate crisps and chopped pecans, for topping (optional)

1. In a large bowl, combine the almond flour, baking powder, xanthan gum, and salt.
2. Line a cake pan that fits inside your air fryer with baking paper.
3. In the bowl of a stand mixer, beat together the butter and powdered sweetener. Add the beaten egg and vanilla and beat for about 3 minutes until smooth.
4. Add the almond flour mixture to the butter and egg mixture and beat until just combined.
5. Stir in the pecans and chocolate crisps.
6. Transfer the dough to the prepared pan and press it into the bottom. Place the cake pan in Zone 1 and Zone 2 of the air fryer baskets, ensuring there's enough space for even cooking.
7. Preheat the Ninja Double Stack Air Fryer to 160°C by selecting the temperature and pressing START/PAUSE to begin. Once preheated, bake the dough for 12 minutes. Remove from the air fryer and let cool for 15 minutes. Using a sharp knife, cut the biscotti into thin strips, then return the strips to the pan with the bottom sides facing up.
8. Preheat the air fryer to 150°C and bake for an additional 8 to 10 minutes until crisp.
9. Once done, remove from the air fryer and let cool completely on a wire rack. If desired, dip one side of each biscotti into melted chocolate crisps and top with chopped pecans.

## Coconut Muffins & Olive Oil Cake

**Prep time: 10 minutes | Cook time: 30 minutes**

**Coconut Muffins | Serves 5**

- 55 g coconut flour
- 2 tablespoons cocoa powder
- 3 tablespoons granulated sweetener
- 1 teaspoon baking powder
- 2 tablespoons coconut oil
- 2 eggs, beaten
- 50 g desiccated coconut

**Olive Oil Cake | Serves 8**

- 60 g blanched finely ground almond flour
- 5 large eggs, whisked
- 175 ml extra-virgin olive oil
- 75 g granulated sweetener
- 1 teaspoon vanilla extract
- 1 teaspoon baking powder

**For Coconut Muffins:**

1. In a mixing bowl, combine all ingredients until well mixed.
2. Pour the mixture evenly into muffin moulds and place them into Zone 1 of the Ninja Double Stack Air Fryer.
3. Select AIR FRY at 180°C and set the timer to 25 minutes. Press START/PAUSE to begin cooking.
4. Once done, check that the muffins are fully cooked by inserting a toothpick into the center; it should come out clean.

**For Olive Oil Cake:**

1. In a large bowl, mix all ingredients until smooth. Pour the batter into an ungreased round nonstick baking dish.
2. Place the baking dish into Zone 2 of the Ninja Double Stack Air Fryer. Select AIR FRY at 150°C and set the timer to 30 minutes. Press START/PAUSE to begin. The cake will be golden on top and firm in the center when done.
3. Allow the cake to cool in the baking dish for 30 minutes before slicing and serving.

## Maple-Pecan Tart with Sea Salt

**Prep time: 15 minutes | Cook time: 25 minutes | Serves 8**

Tart Crust:
- Vegetable oil spray
- 75 g unsalted butter, softened
- 30 g firmly packed brown sugar
- 65 g Plain flour
- ¼ teaspoon kosher, or coarse sea salt

Filling:
- 4 tablespoons unsalted butter, diced
- 60 g packed brown sugar
- 60 ml pure maple syrup
- 60 ml whole milk
- ¼ teaspoon pure vanilla extract
- 190 g finely chopped pecans
- ¼ teaspoon flaked sea salt

1. For the crust: Line two small baking pans with foil, leaving a couple of inches of overhang. Spray the foil with vegetable oil spray.
2. In a medium bowl, combine the butter and brown sugar. Beat with an electric mixer on medium-low speed until light and fluffy. Add the flour and kosher salt, beating until well blended. Divide the crumbly mixture evenly between the prepared pans and press it into the bottom of each pan.
3. Place one pan into Zone 1 and the other into Zone 2 of the Ninja Double Stack Air Fryer. Select AIR FRY for both zones, set the temperature to 180°C, and adjust the timer to 13 minutes. Press MATCH to synchronize and START/PAUSE to begin cooking. While the crusts bake, prepare the filling.
4. For the filling: In a medium saucepan over medium heat, combine the butter, brown sugar, maple syrup, and milk. Bring to a simmer, stirring occasionally. Once simmering, cook for 1 minute, then remove from the heat and stir in the vanilla and pecans.
5. Once the crusts are done, carefully pour the filling evenly over both crusts, gently spreading with a rubber spatula to distribute the nuts and liquid. Return the pans to Zone 1 and Zone 2.
6. Set AIR FRY at 180°C for both zones and adjust the timer to 12 minutes. Press MATCH and START/PAUSE to cook. The filling should bubble, with the center remaining slightly jiggly (it will thicken as it cools).
7. Remove both pans from the air fryer and sprinkle the tarts with sea salt. Allow them to cool completely on wire racks until they reach room temperature.
8. Transfer the pans to the refrigerator to chill. Once cold, use the foil overhang to lift each tart from the pans. Cut into 8 wedges per tart and serve at room temperature.

## Apple Hand Pies

**Prep time: 15 minutes | Cook time: 25 minutes | Serves 8**

- 2 apples, cored and diced
- 60 ml honey
- 1 teaspoon ground cinnamon
- 1 teaspoon vanilla extract
- ⅛ teaspoon ground nutmeg
- 2 teaspoons cornflour
- 1 teaspoon water
- 1 sheet shortcrust pastry cut into 4
- Cooking oil spray

1. Insert the crisper plate into Zone 1 and preheat to 200°C by selecting AIR FRY and pressing START/PAUSE.
2. In a metal bowl that fits into Zone 1, stir together the apples, honey, cinnamon, vanilla, and nutmeg until evenly combined.
3. In a small bowl, whisk the cornflour and water until the cornflour dissolves completely.
4. Once preheated, place the metal bowl with the apple mixture into Zone 1. Cook for 2 minutes, then stir the apples and resume cooking for another 2 minutes.
5. Remove the bowl from Zone 1 and stir in the cornflour mixture. Reinsert the bowl into the basket and cook for an additional 30 seconds until the sauce slightly thickens.
6. Transfer the cooked apple mixture to a refrigerator to cool while preparing the pie crusts.
7. Cut each pie crust into 2 (4-inch) circles, resulting in 8 circles total.
8. Lay the pie crusts on a work surface and divide the apple filling evenly among them, mounding the mixture in the center of each round.
9. Fold each pie crust over so the top layer is about an inch shorter than the bottom layer. Use the back of a fork to seal the edges securely.
10. Insert the crisper plate into Zone 1 and preheat again to 200°C by selecting AIR FRY and pressing START/PAUSE.
11. Once preheated, spray the crisper plate with cooking oil, line Zone 1 with baking paper, and spray it lightly with cooking oil. Working in batches, place the hand pies into Zone 1 in a single layer.
12. Select AIR FRY at 200°C and set the timer to 10 minutes. Press START/PAUSE to cook.
13. When the pies are golden and crisp, allow them to cool for 5 minutes before removing from Zone 1.
14. Repeat steps 11, 12, and 13 with the remaining pies.

# Old-Fashioned Fudge Pie & Chocolate Chip Biscuit Cake

**Prep time: 15 minutes | Cook time: 25 to 30 minutes**

### Old-Fashioned Fudge Pie | Serves 8

- 240 g granulated sugar
- 40 g unsweetened cocoa powder
- 35 g self-raising flour
- 3 large eggs, unbeaten
- 12 tablespoons unsalted butter, melted
- 1½ teaspoons vanilla extract
- 1 (9-inch) unbaked piecrust
- 18 g icing sugar (optional)

### Chocolate Chip Biscuit Cake | Serves 8

- 4 tablespoons salted butter, melted
- 65 g granular brown sweetener
- 1 large egg
- ½ teaspoon vanilla extract
- 55 g blanched finely ground almond flour
- ½ teaspoon baking powder
- 40 g low-carb chocolate crisps

**For Old-Fashioned Fudge Pie:**

1. In a medium bowl, stir together the sugar, cocoa powder, and flour. Add the eggs, melted butter, and vanilla, stirring until the mixture is smooth.
2. Preheat Zone 1 to 180°C by selecting AIR FRY and pressing START/PAUSE.
3. Pour the chocolate filling into the prepared crust and smooth the top.
4. Place the pie into Zone 1. Set AIR FRY to 180°C and the timer to 25 minutes. Stir the filling gently every 10 minutes to ensure even cooking. Press START/PAUSE to begin.
5. Check for doneness by inserting a knife into the center; it should come out clean. If needed, cook for an additional 3 to 5 minutes.
6. Once done, let the pie sit in the basket for 5 minutes before removing. Dust with icing sugar, if desired, and serve warm.

**For Chocolate Chip Biscuit Cake:**

1. In a large bowl, whisk together the butter, sweetener, egg, and vanilla until smooth. Add the flour and baking powder, stirring until the mixture is well combined.
2. Fold in the chocolate crisps, then spoon the batter into an ungreased round nonstick baking dish, spreading it evenly.
3. Place the baking dish into Zone 2 of the Ninja Double Stack Air Fryer. Select AIR FRY, set the temperature to 150°C, and the timer to 15 minutes. Press START/PAUSE to begin cooking.
4. Check for doneness when the edges are browned, indicating the biscuit cake is ready. Remove from Zone 2, slice, and serve warm.

# Strawberry Pastry Rolls

**Prep time: 20 minutes | Cook time: 5 to 6 minutes per batch | Serves 4**

- 85 g low-fat cream cheese
- 2 tablespoons plain yoghurt
- 2 teaspoons granulated sugar
- ¼ teaspoon pure vanilla extract
- 225 g fresh strawberries
- 8 sheets filo pastry
- Butter-flavoured cooking spray
- 45-90 g dark chocolate crisps (optional)

1. In a medium bowl, combine the cream cheese, yoghurt, sugar, and vanilla. Beat with a hand mixer on high speed for about 1 minute until smooth.
2. Wash and destem the strawberries. Chop enough to measure 80 g and stir them into the cream cheese mixture.
3. Preheat both Zone 1 and Zone 2 to 160°C by selecting AIR FRY and pressing MATCH, then START/PAUSE.
4. Filo pastry dries quickly, so cover the stack of sheets with baking paper and a damp dish towel. Remove only one sheet at a time as you work.
5. To make a pastry roll, lay one sheet of filo on a work surface and spray lightly with butter-flavored spray. Top with a second sheet, spraying it lightly as well.
6. Place about 3 tablespoons of filling ½ inch from the edge of the short side. Fold the end over the filling and roll a turn or two. Fold in the left and right sides to seal, then roll up completely. Spray the outside of the roll lightly with butter spray.
7. Once you have prepared 4 rolls, divide them between Zone 1 and Zone 2 of the air fryer, placing them seam-side down and leaving space between each. Select AIR FRY at 160°C for both zones and set the timer to 6 minutes. Press MATCH to synchronize the zones and START/PAUSE to begin cooking.
8. Check the pastries at 5 minutes; if they are golden brown, remove them. Otherwise, cook for 1 more minute. Repeat step 7 for the remaining rolls.
9. Allow the pastries to cool to room temperature.
10. To serve, slice the remaining strawberries. If desired, melt the chocolate crisps in the microwave or a double boiler. Place one pastry on each dessert plate, top with sliced strawberries, and drizzle melted chocolate over the strawberries and onto the plate.

# Coconut Flour Cake & Cream-Filled Sandwich Cookies

**Prep time: 10 minutes | Cook time: 25 minutes**

## Coconut Flour Cake | Serves 6

- 2 tablespoons salted butter, melted
- 35 g coconut flour
- 2 large eggs, whisked
- 100 g granulated sweetener
- 1 teaspoon baking powder
- 1 teaspoon vanilla extract
- 120 ml sour cream

## Cream-Filled Sandwich Cookies | Makes 8 cookies

- Coconut, or avocado oil, for spraying
- 1 tube croissant dough
- 60 ml milk
- 8 Oreos
- 1 tablespoon icing sugar

### For Coconut Flour Cake:

1. Mix all ingredients in a large bowl. Pour the batter into an ungreased round nonstick baking dish.
2. Preheat the Ninja Double Stack Air Fryer to 150°C by selecting the temperature and pressing START/PAUSE to begin. Once preheated, place the baking dish in Zone 1 of the air fryer basket.
3. Bake at 150°C for 25 minutes, or until the cake is dark golden on top. A toothpick inserted in the center should come out clean when done.
4. Once done, let the cake cool in the dish for 15 minutes before slicing and serving.

### For Cream-Filled Sandwich Cookies:

1. Line the air fryer basket in Zone 2 with baking paper and lightly spray with oil.
2. Unroll the dough and cut it into 8 triangles. Lay out the triangles on a work surface.
3. Pour the milk into a shallow bowl. Quickly dip each biscuit in the milk, then place in the center of each dough triangle.
4. Wrap the dough around the cookie, cutting off any excess and pinching the edges to seal. You can combine the excess dough to make additional cookies, if desired.
5. Place the wrapped cookies in the prepared air fryer basket in Zone 2, seam-side down. Spray lightly with oil.
6. Preheat the Ninja Double Stack Air Fryer to 180°C by selecting the temperature and pressing START/PAUSE to begin. Once preheated, bake the cookies for 4 minutes. After 4 minutes, flip the cookies, spray with oil again, and cook for another 3 to 4 minutes, or until puffed and golden brown.
7. Once baked, dust with icing sugar and serve immediately.

# Appendix 1: Basic Kitchen Conversions & Equivalents

### DRY MEASUREMENTS CONVERSION CHART

3 teaspoons = 1 tablespoon = 1/16 cup

6 teaspoons = 2 tablespoons = 1/8 cup

12 teaspoons = 4 tablespoons = 1/4 cup

24 teaspoons = 8 tablespoons = 1/2 cup

36 teaspoons = 12 tablespoons = 3/4 cup

48 teaspoons = 16 tablespoons = 1 cup

## METRIC TO US COOKING CONVERSIONS

### OVEN TEMPERATURES

120 °C = 250 °F

160 °C = 320 °F

180 °C = 350 °F

205 °C = 400 °F

220 °C = 425 °F

### LIQUID MEASUREMENTS CONVERSION CHART

8 fluid ounces = 1 cup = 1/2 pint = 1/4 quart

16 fluid ounces = 2 cups = 1 pint = 1/2 quart

32 fluid ounces = 4 cups = 2 pints = 1 quart = 1/4 gallon

128 fluid ounces = 16 cups = 8 pints = 4 quarts = 1 gallon

### BAKING IN GRAMS

1 cup flour = 140 grams

1 cup sugar = 150 grams

1 cup powdered sugar = 160 grams

1 cup heavy cream = 235 grams

### VOLUME

1 milliliter = 1/5 tsp

5 ml = 1 tsp

15 ml = 1 tbsp

240 ml = 1 cup or 8 fluid ounces

1 liter = 34 fluid ounces

### WEIGHT

1 gram = 0.035 ounces

100 grams = 3.5 ounces

500 grams = 1.1 pounds

1 kilogram = 35 ounces

# Appendix 2: Recipes Index

## A

| | |
|---|---|
| Air Fried Broccoli Bites | 22 |
| Air Fried Butternut Marrow Topped with Hazelnuts | 23 |
| Air Fried Chicken Potatoes with Sun-Dried Tomato | 35 |
| Air Fried Purple Potato Rosemary Chips | 21 |
| Apple Hand Pies | 83 |

## B

| | |
|---|---|
| Bacon, Broccoli and Cheese Bread Pudding | 7 |
| Baked Grouper with Tomatoes and Garlic & Crab Cakes with Peppers | 56 |
| Baked Halloumi with Fresh Greek Topping | 23 |
| Balsamic Tilapia | 49 |
| Banger and Peppers | 39 |
| Beef Bavette Steak with Sage | 40 |
| Beef Burger | 40 |
| Beef Mince Taco Rolls | 40 |
| Beefy Poppers | 46 |
| Berry Muffins | 13 |
| Black Bean Maize Dip & Air Fried Pot Stickers | 62 |
| Blackened Cajun Pork Roast | 47 |
| Bo Luc Lac | 45 |
| Bourbon Vanilla Eggy Bread | 10 |
| Breakfast Meatballs | 5 |
| Broccoli Cheese Chicken | 27 |
| Browned Prawns Patties | 50 |
| Buffalo Cauliflower with Blue Cheese | 70 |
| Buffalo Crispy Chicken Strips | 33 |
| Butter Steak Tips with Potatoes | 17 |
| Buttermilk Breaded Chicken | 27 |
| Buttermilk-Fried Drumsticks | 29 |

## C

| | |
|---|---|
| Cantonese BBQ Pork | 43 |
| Cauliflower, Chickpea, and Avocado Mash & Italian Baked Egg and Veggies | 77 |
| Cheese Pork Chops | 43 |
| Chermoula-Roasted Beetroots & Blistered Shishito Peppers with Lime Juice | 73 |
| Chicken and Gruyère Cordon Bleu | 27 |
| Chicken Breasts with Asparagus, Beans, and Rocket | 29 |
| Chicken Enchiladas | 31 |
| Chicken Pesto Parmigiana | 32 |
| Chicken with Pineapple and Peach | 36 |
| Chiles Rellenos with Red Chile Sauce & Banger-Stuffed Mushroom Caps | 69 |
| Chocolate Chip Pecan Biscotti | 82 |
| Cinnamon Apple Egg Rolls | 16 |
| Cinnamon Rolls | 6 |
| Cinnamon-Apple Crisps & Kale Crisps with Tex-Mex Dip | 64 |
| Cinnamon-Raisin Bagels | 5 |
| Classic Poutine | 60 |
| Classic Prawns Empanadas | 57 |
| Classic Whole Chicken | 28 |
| Coconut Chicken Wings with Mango Sauce | 26 |
| Coconut Flour Cake & Cream-Filled Sandwich Cookies | 85 |
| Coconut Muffins & Olive Oil Cake | 82 |
| Coconut Prawns with Pineapple-Lemon Sauce | 55 |
| Courgette Fritters | 74 |
| Crab Cakes & White Fish with Cauliflower | 56 |
| Crab-Stuffed Avocado Boats | 55 |
| Creamy Mushroom and Green Bean Bake | 16 |
| Crisp Paprika Chicken Drumsticks | 26 |
| Crispy Chorizo-Coated Scotch Eggs | 20 |
| Crispy Dill Chicken Strips | 25 |
| Crispy Filo Vegetable Parcels | 16 |
| Crispy Green Bean Fries with Lemon-Yoghurt Sauce | 61 |
| Crispy Peppery Rice Patties | 20 |
| Crunchy Fish Fingers | 49 |
| Crunchy Tex-Mex Tortilla Chips | 63 |

## D

| | |
|---|---|
| Double-Dipped Mini Cinnamon Biscuits | 9 |

## E

| | |
|---|---|
| Easy Roasted Chickpeas | 61 |
| Egg White Cups | 12 |
| Eggnog Bread | 8 |

## F

| | |
|---|---|
| Fig, Chickpea, and Rocket Salad | 72 |
| Five-Spice Pork Belly | 41 |
| French Garlic Chicken | 32 |
| Fresh Beetroot Salad with Zesty Lemon Dressing | 21 |
| Fried Artichoke Hearts | 65 |
| Fried Chicken Wings with Waffles | 10 |

## G

| | |
|---|---|
| Garlic Cauliflower with Tahini | 75 |
| Garlic Soy Chicken Thighs & Chicken Paillard | 28 |
| Garlic White Courgette Rolls | 78 |
| Gochujang Chicken Wings | 29 |
| Golden Tenders | 34 |
| Greek Chicken Souvlaki | 36 |
| Greek-Style Meatloaf | 45 |
| Green Pepper Cheeseburgers | 39 |
| Grilled Beef Bratwursts | 20 |
| Grilled Steak and Veggie Skewers | 17 |

## H

| | |
|---|---|
| Ham and Cheese Crescents | 12 |
| Ham with Sweet Potatoes | 45 |
| Hearty Blueberry Porridge | 10 |
| Herbed Green Lentil Rice Balls | 64 |
| Honey-Baked Pork Loin | 46 |
| Hush Puppies | 66 |

## I

| | |
|---|---|
| Italian Bangers with Peppers and Onions | 42 |
| Italian Egg Cups | 5 |
| Italian Rice Balls & Fried Dill Pickles with Buttermilk Dressing | 67 |

## J

| | |
|---|---|
| Jalapeño and Bacon Breakfast Pizza | 9 |
| Jalea | 51 |

## K

| | |
|---|---|
| Kale and Potato Nuggets | 9 |
| Korean Flavour Glazed Chicken Wings | 37 |
| Korean Honey Wings | 34 |

## L

| | |
|---|---|
| Lamb Chops with Horseradish Sauce | 42 |
| Lemon Pepper Prawns & Coconut Prawns | 53 |
| Lemon-Basil Turkey Breasts | 26 |
| Lemony Pear Chips & Mixed Vegetables Pot Stickers | 66 |

## M

| | |
|---|---|
| Macadamia Nuts Crusted Pork Rack & Italian Lamb Chops with Avocado Mayo | 44 |
| Maize Croquettes & Garlicky Baked Cherry Tomatoes | 72 |
| Maple-Pecan Tart with Sea Salt | 83 |
| Marinated Salmon Fillets | 55 |
| Mediterranean Creamed Green Peas & Roasted Veggie Bowl | 79 |
| Mississippi Spice Muffins | 6 |
| Mixed Berry Crumble Delight | 15 |
| Mouthwatering Cod over Creamy Leek Noodles | 50 |
| Mushroom-and-Tomato Stuffed Hash Browns | 11 |
| Mustard Herb Pork Tenderloin | 40 |

## N

| | |
|---|---|
| Nutty Muesli | 7 |

## O

| | |
|---|---|
| Oat and Chia Porridge | 11 |
| Oat Bran Muffins | 8 |
| Old-Fashioned Fudge Pie & Chocolate Chip Biscuit Cake | 84 |
| Onion Pork Kebabs | 44 |

## P

| | |
|---|---|
| Pancake Cake | 13 |
| Panko Crab Sticks with Mayo Sauce | 50 |
| Panko Crusted Calf's Liver Strips | 47 |
| Parmesan Ranch Risotto & Frico | 11 |
| Parmesan-Rosemary Radishes | 73 |
| Peachy Chicken Chunks with Cherries | 33 |
| Pecan-Crusted Catfish | 53 |
| Peppered Maple Bacon Knots | 8 |
| Piri-Piri Chicken Thighs | 30 |
| Polenta Casserole | 74 |
| Popcorn Prawns | 49 |
| Pork Kebab with Yoghurt Sauce | 42 |
| Prawns Egg Rolls | 62 |
| Prawns Scampi | 57 |

## Q

| | |
|---|---|
| Quesadillas | 6 |
| Quick and Easy Blueberry Muffins | 7 |

## R

| | |
|---|---|
| Reuben Beef Rolls with Thousand Island Sauce | 43 |
| Roasted Mushrooms with Garlic | 65 |
| Roasted Radishes with Sea Salt & Broccoli-Cheddar Twice-Baked Potatoes | 70 |
| Roasted Vegetable Mélange with Herbs & Vegetable Burgers | 78 |
| Rosemary-Roasted Red Potatoes | 75 |

## S

| | |
|---|---|
| Salmon on Bed of Fennel and Carrot & Cornmeal-Crusted Trout Fingers | 58 |
| Salmon Spring Rolls | 54 |
| Salmon with Cauliflower | 51 |
| Savory Pork Burgers with Tangy Red Cabbage Slaw | 15 |
| Scallops with Asparagus and Peas | 52 |
| Sea Bass with Potato Scales | 54 |
| Sesame Chicken Breast | 31 |
| Short Ribs with Chimichurri | 46 |
| Simple Cheesy Shrimps | 51 |
| Smoky Pork Tenderloin | 47 |
| Snapper with Shallot and Tomato & Garlic Prawns | 52 |
| Soft white cheese Stuffed Jalapeño Chillies Poppers | 61 |
| Southern Chilli | 47 |
| Southwestern Roasted Maize | 74 |
| Spaghetti Zoodles and Meatballs | 41 |
| Spicy Cheesy Jalapeño Cornbread | 21 |
| Spicy Lentil Patties | 65 |
| Spicy Tomato Beef Meatballs | 39 |
| Spinach Cheese Casserole & Greek Baked Beans | 80 |
| Spinach-Artichoke Stuffed Mushrooms | 77 |
| Spiralized Potato Nest with Tomato Tomato Ketchup & Crispy Mozzarella Cheese Sticks | 63 |
| Steak Gyro Platter | 44 |
| Strawberry Pastry Rolls | 84 |
| Stuffed Chicken Florentine | 30 |
| Stuffed Fried Mushrooms | 64 |
| Sugar-Dusted Beignet Treats | 18 |
| Sumptuous Pizza Tortilla Rolls | 41 |
| Super Cheesy Gold Aubergine | 71 |
| Sweet Churro Nuggets | 17 |
| Sweet Tilapia Fillets | 53 |
| Sweet-and-Sour Brussels Sprouts & Cheese-Walnut Stuffed Mushrooms | 71 |

## T

| | |
|---|---|
| Taco-Spiced Chickpeas & Carrot Chips | 60 |
| Tandoori Prawns | 54 |
| Teriyaki Chicken Legs | 25 |
| Thai Chicken with Cucumber and Chili Salad | 35 |
| Turkey and Cranberry Quesadillas | 25 |

## V

| | |
|---|---|
| Veggie Spinach and Carrot Rounds | 22 |
| Veggie Tuna Toasties | 15 |

Made in the USA
Middletown, DE
19 July 2025

10835955R00053